*Fighting
for Uncle Sam*

FIGHTING
for
UNCLE SAM

BUFFALO SOLDIERS *in the* FRONTIER ARMY

JOHN P. LANGELLIER

4880 Lower Valley Road • Atglen, PA 19310

Dedicated to Anthony Powell
and Frank N. "Mickey" Schubert

If the muse were mine to tempt it
And my feeble voice were strong.
If my tongue were turned to measures,
I would sing a stirring song.
I would sing a song heroic
Of those noble sons of Ham,
Of the gallant colored soldiers
Who fought for Uncle Sam!

– Paul Lawrence Dunbar
The Colored Soldiers

Copyright © 2016 by John P. Langellier

Library of Congress Control Number: 2015957317

Cover design by Molly Shields
Type set in Aldine & Arial

ISBN: 978-0-7643-5079-5
Printed in China

Published by Schiffer Publishing, Ltd.
4880 Lower Valley Road
Atglen, PA 19310
Phone: (610) 593-1777; Fax: (610) 593-2002
E-mail: Info@schifferbooks.com

For our complete selection of fine books on this and related subjects, please visit our website at www.schifferbooks.com. You may also write for a free catalog.

This book may be purchased from the publisher. Please try your bookstore first.

We are always looking for people to write books on new and related subjects. If you have an idea for a book, please contact us at proposals@schifferbooks.com.

Schiffer Publishing's titles are available at special discounts for bulk purchases for sales promotions or premiums. Special editions, including personalized covers, corporate imprints, and excerpts can be created in large quantities for special needs. For more information, contact the publisher.

CONTENTS

FOREWORD . . . 7

ACKNOWLEDGMENTS AND ABBREVIATIONS . . . 11

CHAPTER 1
Do you Think I'll Make a Soldier?
African American Fighting Men, 1775–1865
13

CHAPTER 2
Pack Up Your Saddle:
Black Regulars, 1866–1897
35

CHAPTER 3
No Place Like Home:
Garrison Life
77

CHAPTER 4
They Look Like Men: Enlisted Ranks
103

CHAPTER 5
Cadet Gray and Army Blue:
West Point and Officers
139

CHAPTER 6
Christian Soldiers: Chaplains
151

CHAPTER 7
Hot Time in the Old Town: From the Spanish-
American War to Desegregation, 1898–1948
167

CHAPTER 8
Buffalo Soldiers—When Will They
Call You a Man? History and Heritage
For Further Reading
185

REFERANCES . . . 203

INDEX . . . 213

Parsons

1407 MARKET ST.
St. LOUIS, MO

This new cavalry recruit at Jefferson Barracks, Missouri, was ready to head west to "see the elephant" as one of the thousands of blacks who signed on to serve Uncle Sam on the frontier. *George M. Langellier Jr.*

FOREWORD

I first met John Langellier almost fifty years ago. I was in Arizona, researching my doctoral dissertation on African Americans who served in the post-Civil War regular army—the "buffalo soldiers." John was a teenager who already knew a great deal about that army and those soldiers. He also knew a thing or two about hustling and recognized a mark when he saw one. I ended up buying what he claimed was a genuine trooper's overcoat—the kind with the yellow-lined cape that always looked so fine in that trio of John Ford/John Wayne cavalry movies. John got some money and I got a cool look and headed off on an old motorcycle with that cape billowing in the wind. John and I have been on the trail of African American soldiers ever since.

John has an impressive bibliography of books and articles. He swings a wide scholarly rope; subjects he has written about include the many films about George Armstrong Custer, Native American soldiers, illustrated histories of the US Army's combat branches, and a lengthy list of writings on just about every aspect of nineteenth century US military uniforms, arms, and equipment.

There are constants in all of John's writing: a well organized and informative narrative; the presentation of the best period photographs and illustrations; and captions that are extensions of the main text and often read as mini-essays. Reference citations attest to his thorough research of primary and secondary sources. His familiarity with original military documents is another hallmark of his publications.

Fighting for Uncle Sam: Buffalo Soldiers in the Frontier Army fully meets these high standards. It is an excellent general history of the first generation of African Americans serving in the nation's regular army.

PS—I still have the coat—but it no longer fits.

Tom Phillips, PhD, co-author with William Dobak of *The Black Regulars, 1866–1898*

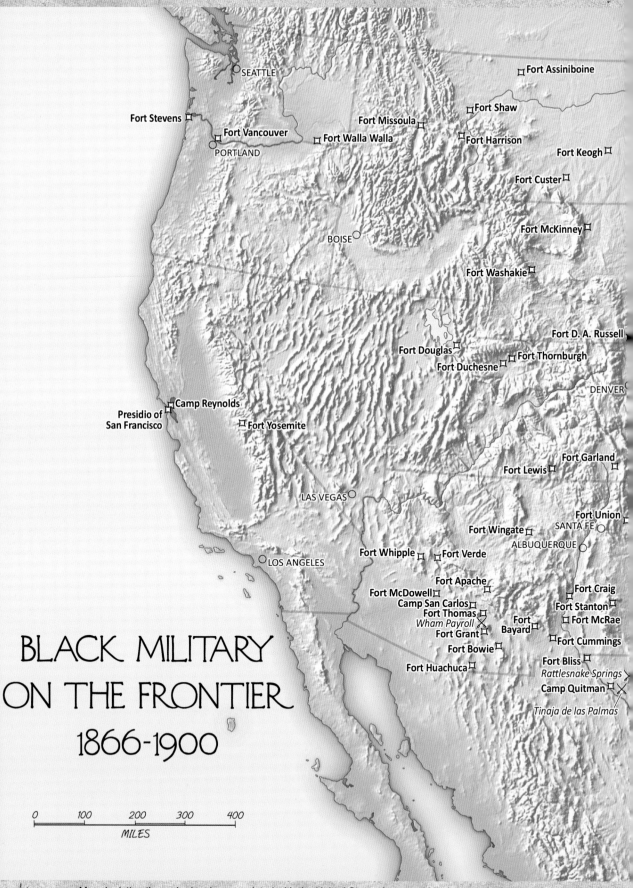

SEATTLE

Fort Stevens

Fort Vancouver

PORTLAND

Fort Walla Walla

Fort Missoula

Fort Shaw

Fort Harrison

Fort Assiniboine

Fort Keogh

Fort Custer

Fort McKinney

BOISE

Fort Washakie

Fort D. A. Russell

Fort Douglas

Fort Duchesne

Fort Thornburgh

DENVER

Camp Reynolds

Presidio of
San Francisco

Fort Yosemite

Fort Garland

Fort Lewis

LAS VEGAS

Fort Union

SANTA FE

Fort Wingate

ALBUQUERQUE

LOS ANGELES

Fort Whipple

Fort Verde

Fort Apache

Fort McDowell

Fort Craig

Camp San Carlos

Fort Stanton

Fort Thomas

Fort McRae

Wham Payroll

Fort
Bayard

Fort Grant

Fort Cummings

Fort Bowie

Fort Bliss

Fort Huachuca

Rattlesnake Springs

Camp Quitman

Tinaja de las Palmas

BLACK MILITARY
ON THE FRONTIER
1866-1900

0   100   200   300   400

MILES

Map depicting the major locales associated with the United States Army and black troops in the
American West, 1866–1900. *Tom Jonas*

Fort Buford

Fort Totten

Fort Rice

Fort Yates

MINNEAPOLIS/ST. PAUL

Fort Snelling

Fort Sully

Fort Hale

Pine Ridge Res.
✕ Wounded Knee   Fort Randall

Fort Robinson   Fort Niobrara

CHICAGO

OMAHA

Fort McPherson

✕ Beecher Island

Fort Leavenworth

Fort Wallace

Fort Hays   Fort Riley

KANSAS CITY

ST. LOUIS

Jefferson Barracks

Fort Harker

Fort Larned   Fort Zarah

Fort Lyon

Fort Dodge   Camp Beecher

Fort Supply

Fort Gibson

Fort Elliot   Fort Reno   OKLAHOMA CITY

Fort Bascom
Palo Duro ✕
Canyon   Fort Sill   Fort Arbuckle

Fort Richardson

Fort Griffin   DALLAS

Fort Concho

Fort Stockton   Fort McKavett

Fort Davis   NEW ORLEANS

Camp Peña Colorado

Camp Hudson   HOUSTON

Fort Clark

Fort Duncan

Fort Ringgold

TOM JONAS, 2015

After two tours of enlistment—as indicated by the service stripes on his lower sleeves—this veteran cavalryman replaced the black regulation campaign hat with a more practical wide brimmed, light-colored piece of headgear. His privately purchased headdress may have been influenced by observing local working cowboys and vaqueros of the era who donned similar hats and in some ways characterized black dandyism, as Monica Miller discusses in her study *Slaves to Fashion*. *Anthony Powell*

ACKNOWLEDGMENTS & ABBREVIATIONS

History, despite its wrenching pain, cannot be unlived,
however, if faced with courage, need not be lived again. —Maya Angelou

While the further reading section found at the conclusion of this book offers some of the best published works to continue exploration of the black military experience in the American West, the over four decades leading to *Fighting for Uncle Sam* also drew on numerous primary sources I reviewed in preparing this text and accompanying illustrations. Consequently, I owe a great debt to several individuals and many institutions.

First and foremost I am grateful to Tom Phillips, Anthony Powell, Frank "Mickey" Schubert, and the late William Leckie for the inspiration they provided and generously sharing information with me. I also wish to thank the Casey Barthelmess family, Rick Collins of the Tucson Presidio Trust, Jerome Greene, Mark Kasal, Tom Jonas, George M. Langellier Jr., the late Herb Peck Jr., and Steve Turner for assistance with this project. In addition, I utilized the resources of the American Heritage Center, Laramie, Wyoming; Arizona Historical Society; Autry Western Heritage Center; Brown University; Denver Public Library; the Fort Huachuca Museum—especially Steve Gregory; Fort Sill Museum; Frontier Army Museum, Fort Leavenworth; Kansas State Historical Society; Moorland-Springarn Research Center, Howard University; Institute of Texan Cultures, San Antonio; Library of Congress (LC); Montana Historical Society; National Archives and Records Administration (NARA); National Park Service; Nebraska State Historical Society; New Mexico Historical Society; Sharlot Hall Museum; Armed Forces History Division, National Museum of American History, Smithsonian Institution; Southern Methodist University; United States Military Academy Library; United States Army Military History Institute; University of Arizona Library Special Collections; University of California Los Angeles Library Digital Collections; University of Montana Mansfield Library; Western Collections, University of Oklahoma Library; University of Vermont; and the Wyoming Historical Society.

During the Revolutionary War, blacks served with both the colonial forces and the British. One of the units fighting for the cause of independence was the First Rhode Island Infantry Regiment, which when first organized included thirty-five freemen and ninety-five men who had been enslaved. Some of these stalwart black patriots served at Yorktown, where French Sublieutenant Jean-Baptiste Antoine de Verger sketched one of these black patriots along with other American troops at that key battle. *Anne K. Brown Collection, Brown University*

Chapter 1

DO YOU THINK I'LL MAKE A SOLDIER?

African American Fighting Men 1775–1865

Even before President Abraham Lincoln's Emancipation Proclamation opened the floodgates, permitting blacks to enlist as federal troops, a field artillery battery formed at Fort Leavenworth in "Bloody Kansas," where just a few years previously John Brown had waged war even before the first shots were fired at Fort Sumter, South Carolina. *Kansas State Historical Society*

"Do you think I'll make a soldier?" is the opening line of one of the old time spirituals originating among enslaved blacks in the South. When this song was written is unknown, but the lyrics raised a long-standing question, because although blacks had a history of bearing arms, their place in the American military was often a matter of differing perspectives. In fact, soon after assuming command of the Continental Army, Virginia slave holder Gen. George Washington ordered that no blacks should be permitted into the military. He supported this position by a council of war and a committee of conference in which representatives from Rhode Island, Connecticut, and Massachusetts agreed with him. Evidently, these founding fathers had forgotten about Crispus Attucks' falling at the Boston Massacre prior to Lexington and Concord.

As the war progressed, Washington and other colonial leaders were compelled by necessity to reverse their ban on blacks. At first blacks fell in with white units, but in due course segregated organizations came into being—perhaps the most noteworthy being a regiment raised in Rhode Island that, at a battle in its home colony, was credited with repulsing three "furious charges of veteran Hessians" (Pickett 1969, 34). According to William H. Chenery's original 1898 pioneering publication *The Fourteenth Regiment Rhode Island Artillery*, "The black regiment was one of three that prevented the enemy from turning the flank of the American army. These black troops were doubtless regarded as the weak spot of the line, but they were not."

When the Revolutionary War closed, black soldiers who had campaigned to create a new nation usually found that the promise of equality and freedom were not meant for them. In some instances, black men who braved battle would be "encased in a cruel and stubborn slavery" rather than enjoy the fruits of their sacrifices (Steward 2014, 64). Even an October 1783 act passed by the Virginia legislature proved very narrow and technical, liberating only those who enlisted by the appointment and direction of their owners who were accepted as substitutes, and who came out of the army with good discharges. So it was that many of those who fought as both a slave and a soldier would—after the Treaty of Paris ended the conflict with the British crown—lay claim to being a veteran but did not gain their freedom.

Despite such unjust treatment, the second war with Great Britain again saw the need for blacks to rally to the Stars and Stripes. Laws were passed—especially in New York—authorizing the formation of regiments of blacks with white officers, a formula that would be repeated elsewhere with few exceptions—such as in New Orleans—and in the future when civil war tore the nation asunder.

The scenario after hostilities commenced between the North and South was a familiar one. At the outset, Abraham Lincoln's administration adopted a ban against blacks taking up arms much as had been the case at the outbreak of the Revolutionary War. Once again, practical and political considerations led to a change of course. Both under black officers at Port Hudson and under white officers on a hundred other battlefields, upwards of 180,000 blacks earned emancipation, rather than just accepting it at the stroke of Lincoln's pen. As

On many levels the Emancipation Proclamation proved the turning point of the Civil War, such as paving the way for official enlistment of blacks as members of the Union Army and Navy. *LC*

Union Adjutant-General Lorenzo Thomas indicated, "Experience proves that they manage heavy guns very well. Their fighting qualities have also been fully tested a number of times, and I am yet to hear of the first case where they did not fully stand up to their work" (Wood c1899, 260).

Maj. Gen. James G. Blunt, writing of the battle of Honey Springs, Arkansas, echoed Thomas when he wrote:

These brothers in arms were among the approximately 180,000 blacks who donned the uniform of Union sailors and soldiers. *LC*

The Negroes [First Colored Regiment] were too much for the enemy, and let me here say that I never saw such fighting as was done by that Negro regiment. They fought like veterans, with a coolness and valor that is unsurpassed. They preserved their line perfect[ly] throughout the whole engagement, and although in the hottest of the fight, they never once faltered. Too much praise cannot be awarded them for their gallantry. The question that Negroes will fight is settled; besides, they make better soldiers in every respect than any troops I have ever had under my command. (Steward 2014, 83)

A hand-tinted photograph of a member of Company B, 103rd Regiment, United States Colored Troops, captures the pride of those blacks who fought for freedom as federal foot soldiers. *LC*

Black Union cavalrymen also took up arms against the South. *LC*

There were artillerymen as well, such as Sgt. Tom Strawn of Company B, Third United States Colored Troops Heavy Artillery Regiment. *LC*

Thousands of black fighting men gave their last full measure in the fight for freedom. Perhaps the black mourning band worn by this proud 1st sergeant was for a fallen comrade, or maybe even for the assassinated commander in chief, who was arguably one of the Civil War's tragic casualties. *LC*

Enlistment often meant leaving loved ones behind when a soldier left to fight for "Father Abraham" against the Confederacy. In some instances photographs might be the only reminder of the many who did not return as a result of disease or combat. *LC*

Gen. Thomas J. Morgan, speaking of the courage of black troops in the battle of Nashville and its effect on Maj. Gen. George H. Thomas, was of like opinion. He indicated:

> Those who fell nearest the enemy's works were colored. General Thomas spoke very feelingly of the sight which met his eye as he rode over the field, and he confessed that the Negro had fully vindicated his bravery, and wiped from his mind the last vestige of prejudice and doubt. (Wood c.1899, 260)

While few blacks received commissions during the Civil War, thousands bore the chevrons of senior non-commissioned officers, as evidenced by the sergeant major on the left and regimental quartermaster sergeant on the right—the top enlisted ranks of the era. *LC*

When the Twentieth United States Colored Troops received their colors on Union Square March 5, 1864, this ceremony must have been a moving one for men who once had been treated as inhuman chattel and now carried the Stars and Stripes with dignity as soldiers. *LC*

Camp William Penn, Pennsylvania, echoed with the marching footsteps of a black regiment that assembled ready to serve as the Union's terrible swift sword. *US Army Military History Institute*

A United States Colored Troops sergeant assumed responsibility during battle and the lulls in between for the men charged to his care. *LC*

Brandishing a Colt percussion revolver, a youthful black infantry private may have wished he could carry this extra firepower into battle in addition to his muzzle-loading rifled musket and bayonet. *LC*

Dressed in overcoats, men of the First Louisiana Guard appear ready for cold weather campaigning, despite the fact they were serving in the Deep South. *LC*

On January 12, 1863, seven companies from a new regiment of African Americans (the Second Louisiana Native Guards) arrived for garrison duty on Ship Island, Mississippi, which had been used as a prison and detention center almost as soon as Union troops landed there. By October 11, 1865, the Second Louisiana Native Guards, which by then had been re-designated the 74th Infantry United States Colored Troops, mustered out of the service and would be replaced by three companies of the 78th United States Colored Troops. *Gulf Islands National Seashore, National Park Service*

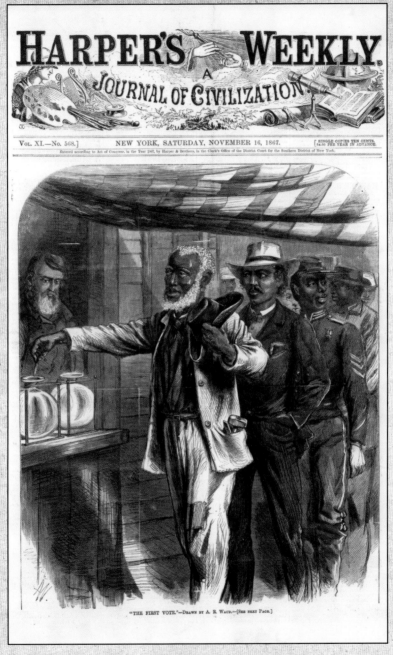

HARPER'S WEEKLY.
A
JOURNAL OF CIVILIZATION.

VOL. XI.—No. 568.]   NEW YORK, SATURDAY, NOVEMBER 16, 1867.   [SINGLE COPIES TEN CENTS.]

"THE FIRST VOTE."—DRAWN BY A. R. WAUD.—[SEE NEXT PAGE.]

The sacrifices of black men who struggled and earned freedom also gave rise to voting rights for black males as the first step toward making good the promise of the Declaration of Independence that "all men are created equal." *LC*

With the Civil War's end black and white veterans could return home knowing they had saved the Union. *LC*

After Robert E. Lee's surrender members of the once-formidable Union Army often met to reminisce and honor their departed fellow veterans as survivors of the 114th Regiment of United States Colored Troops did at a reunion on May 30, 1897, held in Norwich, New York. *LC*

Medals of Honor

The Civil War gave birth to the legendary Medal of Honor. Ultimately, some 1,200 of these prestigious military decorations for valor above and beyond the call of duty would be presented to Union soldiers and sailors, including eighteen men who served in the US Colored Troops (fourteen of whom were recognized for fighting at Chaffin's Farm and New Market Heights, and one to William H. Carney, who served with the famed 54th Massachusetts) and eight black sailors. During the next quarter of a century that followed the Civil War, another eighteen blacks joined this brave band of brothers of the more than 400 men who received the Medal of Honor while serving in the frontier army. (Note: in a number of instances the medals were issued well after the date of the combat action being recognized.)

Twenty-three-year-old William H. Carney of Norfolk, Virginia, volunteered with the storied Fifty-fourth Massachusetts. During the heat of July 18, 1863, while storming Fort Wagner, South Carolina, he grasped the flag from the hands of a wounded color bearer and continued under devastating Confederate fusillades, carrying the regiment's symbol forward during the assault. He became one of the first blacks to receive the Medal of Honor. *LC*

In late September 1864, 1st Sgt. Powhatan Beaty assumed command of his company in Ohio's Fifth Colored Infantry after the commissioned officers were all put out of action during a fierce two-day engagement at Chaffin's Farm, Kentucky. Beaty's bravery under murderous fire resulted in his joining the elite heroes who wore the Medal of Honor. *LC*

Civil War, 1863–1865

Navy

Rating	Name	Date of Issue
Landsman	Aaron Anderson	June 22, 1865
Landsman	Robert Blake	April 16, 1864
Landsman	William H. Brown	August 5, 1864
Landsman	Wilson Brown	December 31, 1864
Seaman	Clement Dees	Deserted before received Medal
Landsman	John Lawson	December 31, 1864
Seaman	Joachim Pease	December 31, 1864
Engineer's Cook	James Mifflin	August 5, 1864

Army

Rank	Name	Date of Issue
Private	William Barnes	April 6, 1865
Private	Powhatan Beaty	April 6, 1865
1st Sergeant	James H. Bronson	April 6, 1865
Private	William H. Carney	May 23, 1900
Sergeant	Decautur Dorsey	November 8, 1865
Sergeant Major	Christian Fleetwood	April 6, 1865
Private	James Gardner	April 6, 1865
Sergeant	James H. Harris	February 18, 1874
Sergeant Major	Milton M. Holland	April 6, 1865
Corporal	James Miles	April 6, 1865
1st Sergeant	Alexander Kelley	April 6, 1865
1st Sergeant	Robert Pinn	April 6, 1865
1st Sergeant	Edward Ratcliff	April 6, 1865
Private	Charles Veal	April 6, 1865

American West, 1866–1890

Army

Rank	Name	Date of Issue
Sergeant	Thomas Boyne	January 6, 1883
Sergeant	Benjamin Brown	February 19, 1890
Sergeant	John Denny	November 27, 1894
Private	Pompey Factor*	
Corporal	Clinton Greaves	Jun 26, 1879
Sergeant	Henry Johnson	September 22, 1890
Sergeant	George Jordon	May 7, 1890
Corporal	Isaiah Mays	February 19, 1890
Sergeant	William McBryar	May 15, 1890
Sergeant	Thomas Shaw	
Private	Adam Payne (aka Paine)*	
Trumpeter	Isaac Payne*	
Sergeant	Emanuel Stance	June 28, 1870
Private	Augustus Walley**	October 1, 1890
Private	John Ward*	
1st Sergeant	Moses Williams	November 12, 1896
Corporal	William O. Wilson	September 17, 1891
Sergeant	Brent Woods	July 12, 1894

*= Seminole Negro Scout **= A recommendation for a second Medal of Honor for actions in Cuba during the Spanish American War was denied.

John Harrison was among the earliest non-commissioned officers in the Tenth United States Cavalry. During the formative years the regiment found it difficult recruiting literate men to handle all the required paperwork. *Southern Methodist University*

Chapter 2

PACK UP
YOUR SADDLE

Black Regulars 1866–1897

Many former black Civil War veterans joined the new infantry
and cavalry regiments established in 1866. *Anthony Powell*

Nearly a year after Robert E. Lee and Ulysses S. Grant met at Appomattox, radical Republicans and others who had championed the cause of blacks entering the ranks of the regular army achieved a milestone. The heretofore exclusive domain of whites—the US Army—would now be open to blacks, albeit on a limited and segregated basis. The proposition of African Americans forming part of the nation's standing peacetime force sparked considerable debate in many forums, including the halls of Congress.

A democratic US senator from California named James Albert McDougall represented one point of view when he contended those who made up the American military, "must belong to the ruling forces...." Classing blacks outside this sphere, McDougall concluded, "this undertaking to place a lower, inferior, different race upon a level with the white man's race, in arms, is against the laws that lie at the foundation of true republicanism." (US *Congressional Globe*, 39th Cong., 1st Sess., 1866, 36: 2, 1385)

Eventually such bigoted opposition on Capitol Hill went down in defeat. In 1866, motivated by a variety of reasons ranging from rewarding officers and the black troops they commanded during their Civil War service or simply to providing employment for large numbers of formally enslaved African Americans, legislators drafted a bill to add six segregated black units to the United States Army. This law brought about the creation of the Ninth and Tenth United States Cavalry regiments, along with the Thirty-eighth, Thirty-ninth, Fortieth, and Forty-first United States Infantry regiments. Three years later, a reorganization of the national martial establishment resulted in the consolidation of the original four outfits of doughboys into two units: the Twenty-fourth and Twenty-fifth United States Infantry regiments, respectively.

For the first time in American military history, blacks attained official permission to enlist in the regular army during peacetime. For the remainder of the nineteenth century, the pair of cavalry and two infantry regiments constituted nearly ten percent of "Uncle Sam's" fighting force on the frontier. Over this period they typically carried out their duties on the frontier, away from the centers of white population, supposedly because of political pressures "to keep blacks from being stationed in northern states to avoid possible racial conflicts" (Steele 1906, 1287). It was one thing to abolish slavery and provide for the vote, but true equality was another matter.

While prejudice operated in the realm of posting, at least the government attempted to be fair when selecting the first officers to lead the new units. Establishing a board to screen white applicants for such service, the panel considered the candidate's record during the Civil War, his capacity for leadership, and other qualifications in an effort to select the best men possible. In general, the choice of officers paralleled the strict criteria established for those who received commissions with the black units during the Civil War. Additionally, the act that created the new units gave preference to men who had commanded African American volunteer units during that conflict.

Wearing the floppy "bummer's" cap and sky blue kersey trousers, this dapper private of Company M was one of the early recruits who signed on with the Tenth US Cavalry during the regiment's formation in the 1860s. *Herb Peck Jr.*

A squad from the Thirty-eighth United States Infantry (later consolidated with the Forty-first Infantry to form the Twenty-fourth) provided protection for a railroad survey crew in post-Civil War Kansas.
Kansas State Historical Society

These high standards had drawbacks. For instance, by the end of 1866, the Tenth United States Cavalry listed only one company-grade officer and two field-grade officers on its rolls. The Tenth still counted only twenty-five officers by the following summer. The other regiments followed a similar pattern. In spite of this situation, no serious effort was made to commission African Americans because in the opinion of one observer from the Fourth United States Cavalry, "... the regiments must be officered by whites else they are of no account" (Parker 1929, 92-93). Nevertheless, three blacks ultimately graduated from West Point during the nineteenth century, while five black chaplains also served at various times after the mid-1880s (see chapters 5 and 6).

Undaunted, the commander of the Tenth United States Cavalry, Benjamin H. Grierson, pressed for personnel. He dispatched Capt. Louis H. Carpenter to Philadelphia, " ... to recruit colored men sufficiently educated to fill the positions of non-commissioned officers, clerks and mechanics in the regiment." The colonel further instructed Carpenter to take, "the greatest care in your selection of recruits ..." so that the rank and file would be "superior men ... who will do credit to the regiment" (Glass 1972, 12-13). Perseverance paid off. By July 1867, Grierson counted 702 of the authorized 1,092 enlisted men of his command.

Evidently some later recruiters ignored Grierson's instructions as to the quality of prospective troopers. For instance, Lt. John Bigelow of the Tenth Cavalry maintained:

> We should have a more honest and generally better class of colored men in the army if our colored regiments were recruited exclusively by officers of those regiments; for, as compared to the general run of officers they are better judges of colored people. How often does one hear a person say that to him or her all negroes are alike. Under that condition of mind, an officer recruiting for a colored regiment takes anybody with kinky hair. (Bigelow 1968, 88)

This same officer complained of missing pieces of horse equipment among his company. He claimed the items disappeared through being lost, as a result of neglect, and because of, "the cardinal vice of the negro, stealing." (Ibid., 88)

While betraying an air of superiority on Bigelow's part, such a condescending attitude was far from unique.

Capt. T. A. Baldwin went so far as to assert blacks had no potential as soldiers because, "The only thing they care for is someone to look after them, they never think for themselves" (Sheffy 1938, 13). In like manner Lt. Col. Eugene Asa Carr, a prominent veteran of many years, voiced what may have been a common belief when he categorically pronounced all blacks unfit for military service. Later, he would have to reconsider these words when a detachment of African American cavalrymen who were escorting Carr drove off an attack by a superior force of American Indians. (King 1963, 77)

During the last quarter of the nineteenth century, enlisted men of the Ninth and Tenth Cavalry regiments wore showy dress uniforms topped by a helmet with a flowing horsetail plume. *Armed Forces History Division, National Museum of American History, Smithsonian Institution*

The recollections of an army officer's wife about her experiences in the immediate post-Civil War era carried similar messages. Frances Roe saw the only advantage of being stationed at a post where blacks were posted was the ease with which one could find "good servants." While Mrs. Roe praised her neighbor's "excellent colored cook" and another Tenth Cavalry trooper who was trained as a "butler" before his enlistment," she found it, "funny ... to see such a black man in a blue uniform." She agreed with her husband that blacks possibly could be "alert and plucky" soldiers, but marred this guarded concession with the verdict, "that they can be good thieves too...." Finally, she expressed outrage over the matter that in a mixed command the "daily mingling of white and colored troops" regularly meant black sergeants were placed "over a white corporal and privates." This situation contradicted the widely held belief of white superiority. (Roe 1981, 65)

Almost three decades later, Marion Brown echoed similar stinging sentiments, noting that at a dress parade she witnessed "a white soldier" being led out "under a colored guard to receive his sentence, or hear it read..." for drunk and disorderly conduct, assault, and resisting arrest. While not appalled by the charges, the young lady was displeased that blacks, rather than whites, had served as the provost; a point that her military host likewise found unacceptable. (King 1970, 59)

Another woman at an army post demonstrated her disdain for African American troops when she succeeded in convincing the officer of the day to place a sergeant and two privates from the Tenth Cavalry in the guardhouse. She complained of their treating her, "with great disrespect, and impertinence...." The regimental commander's spouse, Alice Grierson, countered. She cautioned her husband Benjamin to keep an open mind and hear the soldiers' side of the story before making any judgments on the matter. (Leckie 1989, 24)

Unlike Alice Grierson, Elizabeth Custer held a condescending view of the black soldier. While Libbie's beloved Autie was away she remained at Fort Riley, which she portrayed in a harsh light:

> You should see this post! It is, everyone says, the most thoroughly run-down and utterly uncared for and shiftless place they ever saw. The one darkey bugler sounds every call on the board—at least, at the hour of every call the cavalry used to hear, the bugler toots something so absurd, and as much like the true call as a cow's low. Shots are fired constantly. You should have seen the parade ground this afternoon! It would have driven an officer given to order and discipline to the verge of distraction. His "black-faced and shiney-eyed" were drilling right on the grass of the parade ground, which is just beginning to show itself green. While the sergeant drilled one squad, another rolled on the ground like apes.... Really, if I were not afraid, these things would be funny. A lieutenant was passing the guardhouse when a negro sentinel called out, "Turn out the guard for commanding officer!" He was full of amusement, but only said quietly, "Never mind the guard," and then hurried up to laugh with us about their so saluting a lieutenant.... (Custer 1889, 536-37)

Such stinging descriptions must have met with George A. Custer's approval. As noted in the collections of the Thomas Gilcrease Institute, Tulsa, OK, "The Boy General" refused a position in a black regiment because he did not want to serve with African Americans; one of the few points on which he and his subordinate, Capt. Frederick W. Benteen, agreed. (F.W. Benteen to T.W. Golden, October 20, 1891)

Some other officers would accept an assignment to a black regiment only if inducements were provided, believing that such a posting might adversely impact their careers. An advertisement in *The Army and Navy Journal*—the influential military periodical of the period—summed up this attitude:

> A first lieutenant of Infantry (white) stationed at a very desirable post in the Department of the South desires a transfer with an officer of the same grade, on equal terms if in a white regiment; but if a colored regiment, a reasonable bonus will be expected. (*Army and Navy Journal*, June 10, 1871, 684)

More overt discrimination was apparent when the Tenth arrived at Fort Leavenworth. In 1866, that post's commander, William Hoffman, quartered the outfit in the swampy lowlands of the installation. Hoffman withheld permission for Grierson to relocate the outfit to another area of the reservation. Additionally, Hoffman ignored Grierson's petition to provide wooden walkways through the mire that surrounded the cavalrymen. As a result health deteriorated. Many succumbed to pneumonia. An outbreak of cholera followed and compounded the hardships. Under the circumstances, Grierson trained his command as rapidly as possible, then sent out his companies to Fort Riley, Kansas, and later to Indian Territory, to be closer to the action. This move thereby allowed the command to escape Hoffman's heavy-handedness.

Even then, the troopers were not immune to ill treatment. At Fort Larned, Kansas, "An incident at the sutler's store in December, 1868, almost resulted in a race riot." During the following month at that post, the stable for the black cavalrymen's horses went up in flames, killing thirty-nine mounts and destroying considerable government property. The fire was, "Believed to have been a case of arson...." (Oliva 1988, 51)

While discrimination plagued the black soldiers, racial slurs and injustice did not keep them from becoming "first-rate regiments and major forces in promoting peace and advancing civilization along America's last continental frontier" (Leckie 1967, 260). A quarter of a century of continuous assignments on the Great Plains, in western mountains, and southwestern deserts developed them into seasoned veterans, as brief histories of each unit indicate.

For instance, the Ninth United States Cavalry—organized in Greenville, Louisiana, in August 1866—drew most of its original recruits from nearby New Orleans, with a few from Kentucky. Col. Edward Hatch, the regimental commander, spent the next seven months completing the unit's formation. He faced a formidable task. While the recruits poured in, the officers did not. Without officers, new conscripts could not be adequately trained and disciplined. Ignoring the unit's lack of officers and insufficient training, orders came in March 1867 for all twelve companies (with a total strength of 885 men) of the Ninth Cavalry to set out for San Antonio, Texas. While en route mutiny erupted among the troops, leaving one officer and two enlisted men dead.

Hatch urgently pleaded with his superiors for additional officers immediately following this fatal episode. His request was approved and the regiment rapidly received additional officers. With this action the regiment would be on the move again. After only two months in San Antonio, word came to head to new assignments at forts farther west. Two companies had already taken up duty at Brownsville. The remaining ten companies received orders to occupy Forts Stockton and Davis along the Texas-Mexico border.

Hatch established the regimental headquarters at Fort Stockton, along with four companies. His second-in-command, Lt. Col. Wesley Merritt, led the other six companies at Fort Davis.

The Ninth Cavalry remained in Texas for the next eight years. Their primary missions were to protect the mail and stage route from San Antonio to El Paso, establish law and order in the border region, and prevent Indian raids.

These were no easy tasks. During the Civil War, west Texas had degenerated into a state of lawlessness. Many of the Texas forts had been abandoned, first by the Union army and later by the Confederates. Mescalero Apaches from the west, Kiowa and Comanches from the north, and Kickapoos and Lipans from Mexico all took advantage of the disarray among Americans and sought vengeance upon the white settlers and reclaim as much of their former lands as possible. The region's lack of law enforcement also attracted bandits, thieves, and rustlers from both sides of the border, while foreign powers had taken advantage of the clash between blue and gray to establish a puppet ruler—Emperor Maximilian— to rule over Mexico. This last action increased unrest along the international boundary between the United States and its southern neighbor. Lawlessness and chaos followed.

The army aggravated the situation by assigning only three cavalry regiments to Texas: the Fourth, Sixth, and Ninth. Of these three, only the Ninth served continuously in the region. The other two regiments spent much of their time serving as occupation forces in the more populated regions of the state during Reconstruction. Even if all three regiments had been posted to the Texas frontier, the area still was too vast and the American Indians too numerous for effective patrolling. To make their duty even more difficult, the Ninth Cavalry faced continuing societal prejudice. Although the settlers in Texas desperately needed protection from Indians and others, they did not welcome black soldiers.

During the summer of 1867—when the Ninth Cavalry arrived in west Texas— they were unprepared for the duty awaiting them. The Indians' lightning fast raids surprised the raw recruits. For the first several months they had little success

A Ninth United States Cavalry plate for the regulation dress helmet worn by all troopers, 1881–1902. *George M. Langellier Jr.*

in thwarting Indian attacks. However, toward the end of 1867, Company K engaged nearly 1,000 Kickapoos, Lipans, and Mexicans at abandoned Fort Lancaster. Although outnumbered 12 to 1, the black troopers managed to drive off the attackers, killing at least twenty warriors and wounding many. The black unit suffered only three casualties in the unbridled skirmish.

For the next seven years, the Ninth Cavalry engaged in scores of fire fights. Only during the coldest part of winter (which lasted about two months) did the Indian raids and outlaw activity subside. The remainder of the year Texas was beset by small war parties. To protect as much territory as possible, at one time or another members of the Ninth Cavalry occupied virtually every fort along the west Texas frontier. After the attack at Fort Lancaster, the two companies at Brownsville relocated farther north along the Rio Grande to Forts Duncan and Clark. Abandoned Fort Quitman—northwest of Fort Davis—was reactivated and also garrisoned by elements of the Ninth Cavalry.

As the troopers of the Ninth became familiar with both the harsh elements of west Texas and their enemies' tactics, they had more success intercepting the raiders and chasing them down. Unfortunately for the black soldiers, the proximity of the Mexican border offered advisories a nearby sanctuary. Knowing that United States cavalrymen were prohibited from crossing the Rio Grande, the raiders, when closely pursued, invariably fled into Mexico. It became obvious that more drastic means were necessary to curb Indian raids. Upon his return as commander of the Ninth in September 1869 after eighteen months of detached service with the Freedman's Bureau in Louisiana, Col. Hatch launched an all-out campaign to clear the region of a determined foe.

By this time the troopers of the Ninth Cavalry were combat-hardened veterans and anxious to take the offensive against their elusive enemy. In January 1870, in the height of winter, members of the Ninth Cavalry marched out of Fort Davis and into Apache territory. For the following five months, the men of the Ninth chased the Mescalero Apaches west into New Mexico, killing relatively few but destroying many of their lodges and capturing their horses. During this campaign Sgt. Emanuel Stance of Company F earned the Congressional Medal of Honor.

While the spring 1870 campaign was largely successful removing the Mescaleros from west Texas, the Kiowas, Comanches, Kickapoos, and Lipans remained in the area. It was believed the only way to subdue the Kickapoos and Lipans was to pursue them back to their villages in Mexico. In December 1870, Col. Hatch sought permission from the United States and Mexican governments to cross the Rio Grande. Washington complied with the request, but President Benito Juárez, who after assuming the reins of Mexico from the ousted Maximilian struggled to maintain his presidency against Gen. Porforio Diáz, refused. Without the ability to pursue war parties into Mexico, the detachments of the Ninth experienced only limited success controlling these tribes.

Also hamstringing the efforts of the Ninth Cavalry was continuing racial hostility and lack of cooperation from local authorities. The situation became so intolerable that in May 1875, Secretary of War William Belknap threatened Texas Governor Richard Coke with withdrawal of all federal troops from his state if he did not curb the racial hostility against black troops. Whether or not Governor Coke improved conditions for black troops, the army decided to transfer the Ninth Cavalry. Its new assignment was the Department of New Mexico, a region fraught with hardships and problems similar to those in Texas.

In eight years of service in some of the most rugged and hostile territory in the country, the Ninth Cavalry engaged in almost constant conflict with American Indians, Mexican revolutionaries, and outlaws. The main challenge could be traced to a diverse, formidable group known to the whites as Apaches. Many of these independent-minded inhabitants of the Southwest resisted efforts by the federal government to isolate them in this barren and desolate region. Faced with the choice of either remaining on the reservations and starving to death or leaving their compound and facing the wrath of the United States Army, many bands of Apaches fled to Mexico. Meanwhile, the United States punished those who stayed behind by attempting to consolidate them to the hated confines at San Carlos, Arizona, and other reservations in that territory and neighboring New Mexico. These actions only increased Apache defiance. They began raiding at will throughout the region.

In late 1875, the Ninth Cavalry received orders transferring the regimental headquarters to Santa Fe, New Mexico. For the next six years, the regiment was scattered at posts throughout the region, including Forts Bayard, McRae, Wingate, Stanton, Union, Selden, and Garland. Their primary mission was to subdue the uncooperative American Indians and respond to trouble within the reservations. As hardened veterans of Indian warfare in Texas, the Ninth Cavalry were placed on patrol, pursuing Apaches who had bolted. Unfortunately for the black soldiers, they were forced to fight the Indians with only half their authorized strength (the remaining number not being assigned to the field). As in Texas, the Ninth Cavalry was spread across too much territory and was severely undermanned.

Their first significant encounter with the American Indians came in September 1877, when 300 Apache warriors led by Victorio fled the San Carlos reservation and began strikes along the Upper Gila River. The Ninth Cavalry closed with Victorio and his band in the Mogollon Mountains. Within a month they forced the Apaches to surrender and return to the San Carlos reservation. Not long after the black troops left, Victorio and his men quickly returned to raiding and pillaging. Again, the Ninth Cavalry responded. In February 1878, the black troops surrounded a party at Ojo Caliente. In subsequent negotiations, Victorio and his followers agreed to surrender on the condition they would not be forced to return to San Carlos. But this would not be the last encounter with Victorio.

During their six-year stint in the New Mexico Territory, the Ninth Cavalry did more than just subdue rebellious Apaches. They were also involved in tempering a number of civil disputes. One of these details took place in December 1887, in the vicinity of El Paso, where a "salt war" erupted between Americans and Mexicans who made similar claims to the salt deposits east of the border town. The dispute led to all-out rioting in nearby San Elizario, resulting in nearly a dozen deaths. Texas Governor Richard Coke was forced to request federal assistance to quell the uproar. The arrival of nine troops from the Ninth Cavalry quickly quieted the rioters. (Cool 2008)

The following summer, the Ninth Cavalry again rode into the fray, this time in Lincoln County, New Mexico, to restore order in the McSween and Murphy-Dolan feud; the most famous participant was William Bonney, also known as Billy the Kid. For months, troopers from the Ninth Cavalry chased down the outlaws during a period of violence.

Meanwhile, the Ninth was faced with a new trial— Utes from Colorado. In 1868, the Utes agreed to remove themselves to a reservation in western Colorado. During the 1870s silver boom there were boundary disputes between Utes and miners. Following Colorado's entrance into the Union in 1876, whites pushed the federal government to remove the Utes from their silver-laden land. While officials in Washington pondered the request, squatters moved onto the Ute reserve. The Utes naturally resisted and took up arms to protect their rights. In March 1878, members of the Ninth Cavalry entered the southern border of the Ute reservation. Col. Hatch managed to quell the possible outbreak without resorting to force. He then successfully negotiated an agreement between the two parties that provided white settlers with a small strip of land from the Ute reservation.

Other elements of the Ninth Cavalry were not so fortunate in their encounter with the White River Utes the following year. Trouble began when federal Indian agent Nathan Meeker wanted to force the nomadic Utes to become farmers. The Utes resisted this new lifestyle and threatened to revolt. Meeker immediately asked for military support and the army complied with his request, sending the Third and Fifth Cavalry and Fourth Infantry. When the troops crossed the Milk River on September 29, 1878, the Utes attacked. Later that day, Company D of the Ninth Cavalry received an urgent request for assistance. Capt. Francis Dodge and his command saddled up their mounts and marched continuously for twenty-three hours to reach the Milk River, where they found the troops pinned down. For three days the soldiers held off the Utes. Finally, on October 5, white troopers from the Fifth United States Cavalry arrived from Fort D. A. Russell, giving the Americans the needed manpower to overwhelm the outnumbered Utes. As a result of his actions during the conflict, Sgt. Henry Johnson of the Ninth was awarded the Congressional Medal of Honor.

The smoldering Ute situation had barely been extinguished when during 1879–1880, Victorio once again required the Ninth (and Tenth) Cavalry to take to the field. In late August 1879, Victorio led a group of Mescalero Apaches off the reservation to raid sheepherders and generally wreak havoc among the white population. On September 4, his strike force made a daring attack against Company E of the Ninth Cavalry at Ojo Caliente, killing eight guards and stealing forty-six horses. The Ninth Cavalry quickly responded, sending virtually every man to search out and destroy Victorio's band. They chased the Apaches, even following them across the border into Mexico. Only when they had exhausted their supplies did the black troops return to Fort Bayard, New Mexico.

Victorio remained in Mexico. The Apaches finally caught the ire of the Mexican army when they killed over two dozen civilians in two separate attacks at Carrizal. In January 1880, Victorio and his men beat a hasty retreat across the border, taking refuge in the San Andres Mountains.

The following month, Colonel Hatch traveled south from the regimental headquarters in Santa Fe to take charge of the campaign against Victorio. Suspecting that Victorio obtained supplies from the Mescalero Apaches on the Tularosa Reservation, Hatch's first move was to disarm and dismount the inhabitants of this reservation. This action only angered the Apaches, compelling between thirty and fifty to join Victorio's followers. The Mescalero Apaches were not the only ones receiving reinforcements: five troops from the Tenth, two troops from the Sixth Cavalry, and two Indian scout companies arrived from Texas and Arizona to assist the Ninth Cavalry.

Before the strike force mobilized, Victorio and his band escaped from the San Andres Mountains and sought sanctuary in their former homeland, near the Mogollon range in western New Mexico. Throughout May 1880, the Ninth Cavalry exhausted themselves chasing Victorio through the Mogollon and Black Mountains as far west as San Carlos. When they finally closed in on the band at the end of the month, Victorio fled across the border into Mexico. Because of his attacks against citizens of Carrizal the previous year, the Mexicans were also anxious to bring Victorio to bay. By crossing the border Victorio had, in essence, jumped out of the frying pan and into the fire. In October, Mexican troops trapped Victorio and his men in a mountain canyon. Refusing to surrender, the Apaches made a gallant, yet suicidal attempt to shoot their way out of the snare. Victorio and sixty of his followers perished.

Although Victorio was dead, his legacy lived. In October 1880, a surviving group of his followers led by Nana (Victorio's former lieutenant) continued to raid southern New Mexico. For the next year, troopers of the Ninth Cavalry chased small raiding parties in and out of New Mexico mountains and back and forth across the Mexican border. They continued this grueling campaign until they were relocated out of New Mexico late in 1881. Nana and his men eventually shifted westward into Arizona.

After nearly fourteen years of continuous warfare in the southwest, the Ninth Cavalry finally received relief from frontier duty and was sent to the relatively quiet solitude of Kansas and Oklahoma Territory. Regimental headquarters went to Fort Riley, Kansas, with various troops posted at Forts Elliott, Hays, Sill, Reno, and Supply. In their new assignment, the cavalrymen spent more time than ever before in garrison, but they also faced new assignments.

In the 1880s, the Oklahoma Territory was still used by the federal government as a reservation for more than a dozen different Indian tribes. Whites were prohibited by law from entering the Indian Territory. This restriction did not stop invasion of the Indians' domain. Between 1879 and 1881, alarming numbers of settlers began filtering into today's Oklahoma. The Ninth Cavalry was called on to defend Indian lands by removing squatters. Whites in the region quickly grew to detest the black cavalrymen.

One former soldier, pioneer, adventurer, and would-be colonizer named David L. Payne proved particularly troublesome to members of the Ninth Cavalry. Recognized as the leader of the "Oklahoma Movement" (an unofficial organization designed to promote settlement of Oklahoma), Payne brazenly made four forays into Indian Territory in 1882 to try and establish a colony; each time he was arrested and escorted out of the region.

With each successive attempt, Payne and his followers (known as "Boomers") became more determined to return and stay. In August 1882, the situation reached a critical point when the squatters refused to pack up their wagons and leave. Just as determined to perform their duty, the troopers of the Ninth loaded the Boomers' belongings, hog tied them, and tossed them into their wagons before driving them out of the Indian Territory. This treatment apparently only stiffened Payne's resolve. In January 1883, he came back with over 900 settlers. Again, the cavalrymen arrested Payne (only temporarily) and escorted the would-be colonizers back to Kansas. In June the following year, Payne made another abortive attempt to colonize the Indian Territory, but this venture proved no different than previous ones. While organizing one more group of filibusters to invade Oklahoma in 1884, Payne suddenly died.

Payne's death did not dampen the Boomers' dream of a colony in Oklahoma. William Couch, one of Payne's most forceful followers, took over the Oklahoma Movement. On at least three occasions during the second half of 1883, Couch led the Boomers to Oklahoma. Each time, members of the Ninth Cavalry escorted them out of the Indian Territory. With each encounter the squatters became more reluctant to leave, increasing the probability of a bloody confrontation that nearly became a reality in January 1885. Couch and 300 settlers encamped on Stillwater Creek ignored Colonel Hatch's mandate to leave. To compel the Boomers, Hatch assembled seven companies of the Ninth, a company of infantry, and two howitzers, and threatened to attack the encampment. The squatters still refused to obey and promised to defend themselves from forcible removal. Desiring to avoid bloodshed, Hatch decided to surround the camp and cut off their supplies. Within five days the siege caused the Boomers to return to Arkansas City.

After nearly four years of performing the thankless, unpopular service of controlling white encroachment, the war department transferred the Ninth Cavalry to the Department of the Platte. During their stay in Kansas and the Indian Territory, the Ninth never participated in combat; instead, they spent most of their time in garrison and on routine patrols. The reason for their transfer remains unclear: there was no pressing demand for troops in Nebraska, while there was a continuing need for them in the Indian Territory —at least until the area was opened for settlement in 1889. Perhaps the racial tension between white settlers and black troopers convinced army officials that the job was best left to white soldiers. In any case, the Ninth Cavalry moved again.

During June 1885, the regiment took up various posts throughout the upper plains with regimental headquarters at Fort Robinson, while assorted companies were stationed at Fort Duchesne in Utah, Fort McKinney in Wyoming, and Fort Niobrara in Nebraska. Headquarters frequently shifted troops from one post to another, but the general trend was consolidating regiments in one or two forts. By 1896, troops from the Ninth Cavalry were stationed only at Forts Robinson

In 1883, an escort of black troopers apprehended David L. Payne and his fellow "Boomers" who moved into Indian lands in today's Oklahoma. These interlopers were to be returned to Kansas under guard. The middle photograph possibly includes David L. Payne standing third from the left. *Western Collections, University of Oklahoma Library*

Troops of the Ninth United States Cavalry on dress parade at Fort McKinney, west of Buffalo, Wyoming Territory, 1890s, including the troop's 1st sergeant, Jeremiah Jones, who is in front of the unit to the far right of the photo—the position of authority for the top non-commissioned officer of the outfit. *American Heritage Center, Laramie, Wyoming*

Cpl. Clarence Grant Morledge of the Ninth United States Cavalry deployed to Pine Ridge Reservation in response to the unrest that erupted during the Ghost Dance movement among the Lakota (Sioux). *Nebraska State Historical Society*

and Duchesne. With the closing of the frontier near the turn of the century, the West became much more peaceful. Except for a few explosive incidents, the Ninth's years in the Department of the Platte reflected this tranquility.

The Ninth Cavalry's "one last moment of glory" was participation in the tragic Lakota (Sioux) Ghost Dance uprising during the summer of 1890. The winter of 1889–1890 was particularly harsh and the Lakota Indians—confined to six small reservations in North and South Dakota—suffered miserably. Impoverished, hungry, and sick, the Lakota needed only a foretelling of a future utopia devoid of whites to spark unrest. This rumor originated from a Paiute named Wovoka, who preached of a new world in which the Indians "would be reunited with dead friends and relatives in a blissful and eternal life, free of pain, sickness, want, and death, free, above all, of white people" (Utley 1973, 412). Through intense prayer and the physically exhausting "Ghost Dance," the Lakota were supposedly able to glimpse into this promised new world. Soon religious fervor swept throughout the Lakota camps.

The movement might have passed peacefully except for two unfortunate events. First, the Bureau of Indian Affairs replaced the agent at the Pine Ridge reservation with one lacking experience in Indian relations. This new agent, D.F. Royer, overreacted to the frenzied dancing and chanting and requested troops. In late November 1890, five companies of the Ninth Cavalry, along with eight companies from the Second and Eighth United States Infantry, arrived at Pine Ridge and Rosebud reservations. The presence of the 600 troops alarmed the Lakota, who quickly divided into two groups: those who wished to comply with the soldiers and others intent on defying them. The recalcitrant Lakota withdrew to a remote area in the northwest corner of the Pine Ridge reservation. By early December, approximately 600 Lakota families from Pine Ridge and Rosebud had joined them.

To prevent a situation similar to the one at Pine Ridge occurring at the other Lakota reservations, Gen. John R. Brooke ordered the arrest of the two most influential Lakota chiefs: Sitting Bull and Big Foot. This course of action turned out to be the federal government's second and most damaging mistake.

After his arrest by Indian police, Sitting Bull's followers attempted to rescue their leader. The venture failed miserably, resulting in the deaths of Sitting Bull, six Lakota warriors, and an equal number of Indian police. In response, the leaders at Pine Ridge reservation invited Big Foot (who was still under military observation) to come and help restore peace. The military was unaware of this invitation. When Big Foot left the reservation they misunderstood his intentions and troopers from the Ninth and Seventh Cavalry regiments were dispatched to retrieve him. Two companies of the Seventh Cavalry eventually located Big Foot and his entourage and began escorting them to Pine Ridge. When the rest of the Seventh Cavalry closed with them at Wounded Knee Creek, the commander ordered the Lakota to hand over their weapons. The warriors refused. What resulted was the tragedy known as the massacre at Wounded Knee.

During early 1869, troopers of the Tenth United States Cavalry scouted the area around Medicine Bluff Creek in today's Oklahoma, where they would establish Fort Sill. This post remains in operation as one of the oldest army garrisons in the West. *Fort Sill Museum*

August 2, the same company and ninety men of the Eighteenth Kansas Cavalry (a volunteer unit) came under fire again; one black trooper and two of the volunteers were killed. Cheyenne casualties are unknown.

In rapid succession soldiers of the Tenth Cavalry fought in three more skirmishes before the end of the year: two with Cheyenne and one with Comanche. These fights revealed a lack of training among the newly enlisted cavalrymen, but also demonstrated their bravery and willingness to follow orders. Elements of the Tenth likewise participated in Gen. Philip Sheridan's 1867–68 winter campaign against Black Kettle's band of Cheyenne.

In November 1867, Colonel Grierson shifted Company M south into Indian Territory, posting the unit at Fort Gibson. During this time the soldiers in Indian Territory experienced no combat, but were busy nonetheless. Occupied with monotonous garrison routines, it must have been frustrating for the soldiers of the Tenth Cavalry. Time and again news of the occasional Indian raid, the illegal whiskey trade, or the theft of cattle and horses reached them, but the perpetrators typically made good their escape.

For most of 1868, peace reigned on the Great Plains. In late 1867, the Comanche, Kiowa, Kiowa-Apache, Southern Cheyenne, and Arapaho signed the Medicine Lodge treaties. Unfortunately, the United States Senate battled internally over the details of the treaties, delaying their ratification and implementation. As 1868 wore on the tribes grew increasingly upset with the United States' apparent failure to honor their promises. Groups of Indians gathered at various Indian agencies throughout the area, expecting the supplies guaranteed to them. When the Indian agents told them they had little to offer the Indians responded with raids. In May, a band of Comanche made a major raid on the Wichita Indian Agency, burning it to the ground.

In late summer, the United States Congress finally appropriated the funds to implement the Medicine Lodge treaties. Disbursal of the annuities to the Indians began during the first week of August 1868. Regrettably, the government made the mistake of including firearms and ammunition (for use in hunting game) as part of the payment. Instead, the Indians used the weapons to attack white settlers in Kansas. This response prompted the government to initiate a policy forcing all Indians south of the Kansas border into Indian Territory. Those who refused to move were to be killed.

Troopers of the Tenth Cavalry saw a great deal of combat in implementing this policy. As the Indian attacks continued to increase, Gen. Sheridan made plans for a decisive campaign that winter.

The Tenth Cavalry played a variety of roles during this campaign. In November 1868, three companies were sent to Fort Cobb to keep an eye on the nearby Kiowa and Comanche. Although these Indians had not participated in any of the fighting, they were reported to be "sullen and restless." Company E remained at Fort Arbuckle, while four other companies patrolled the Kansas border and another four moved to Fort Lyon. The companies at Fort Lyon did not see any combat, but made long marches under blizzard conditions that kept the various tribes from moving north or west. The troopers stationed in Indian Territory experienced the same blizzard conditions, but also engaged the Indians.

The 1868–69 winter campaign on the Great Plains was successful. As a result, the entire Tenth Cavalry headed into Indian Territory early. In January 1869, several companies arrived at the site on Medicine Bluff Creek and began constructing temporary shelters. The new post was named Camp Wichita and regimental headquarters was transferred there in March. Permanent construction began shortly thereafter. The camp was renamed Fort Sill in August. By that time, the regiment was divided between Fort Sill and Camp Supply, with six companies at each post. For the next six years the Tenth Cavalry remained in Indian Territory, acting as an army of occupation among the various American Indian tribes removed to the reservations. They were charged with keeping the local Indian population on the reservations and prohibiting the entry of whites on to Indian lands. Various companies were stationed at Forts Dodge, Gibson, Arbuckle, Sill, and Supply, and at the Cheyenne Indian Agency to accomplish these duties.

Interdicting movements off the reservations proved difficult and kept the black troops patrolling the Red River, hoping to intercept groups returning to the reservations, scouting for trespassers, and continuing construction of the fort. Fort Sill was attacked only occasionally. More frequently, Army brass deemed a show of force necessary and ordered the Tenth Cavalry to patrol the field, periodically for weeks at a time.

In June 1872, the Army transferred the Tenth Cavalry's headquarters back to Fort Gibson, responding to an increase in the number of white intruders into Indian Territory from the north. Regimental headquarters returned to Fort Sill less than a year later, where it remained until March 1875. During those years the regiment was divided between Indian Territory and Texas. In April 1873, the Army ordered companies south into Texas: three companies were stationed at Fort Richardson, two at Fort Griffin, and two at Fort Concho. The companies remaining in Indian Territory were concentrated at Fort Sill and Camp Supply. The Indian Territory remained relatively quiet during the summer of 1873, although small raiding parties continued to harass the north Texas border. The black troopers spent most of the summer in the saddle scouting for these raiders, but saw little action.

Winter did not bring the expected respite from field duty. Kiowa and Comanche raids into Texas were so frequent that the Tenth Cavalry spent the cold months stationed at a string of stockaded camps between Forts Sill and Griffin to more quickly intercept raiding parties. Bellicose activity increased through the spring and summer. By July, military leaders planned another major campaign against the Kiowa and Comanche, similar to the one of 1867–68. Troopers took to the field in September and remained there until the following spring. During this campaign known as the Red River War, five columns were formed from regiments stationed in the Departments of Texas and Missouri, with the Tenth Cavalry providing the backbone of one of these columns. After enduring the winter of 1874–1875 mostly in the saddle, the regiment moved back south to Texas.

In April 1875, the entire regiment was stationed in Texas, with regimental headquarters remaining at Fort Concho. Six companies moved into Fort Concho, with two each at Forts Griffin and McKavett and one each at Forts Davis and Stockton. The seven companies that were moved south into Texas two years earlier remained as busy as the troopers in the Indian Territory. West Texas in 1873 was a barely settled region, with frontier towns comprised mostly of transients. In addition to preventing and responding to Apache raids, the troopers' duties included escorts for contractor trains and stages, and assisting civilian authorities capturing rustlers and other criminals.

After the regiment was reunited in April 1875, it was destined to remain in Texas for the next decade. Regimental headquarters continued at Fort Concho for seven of those years. The various companies of the regiment would be scattered over the length and breadth of western Texas for protection of the frontier. Their pursuits of small bands of Indians kept detachments in the field for many long marches over a great expanse of harsh land, from the north border of Texas across the Rio Grande into Mexico.

In July 1875, six companies of the Tenth Cavalry took part in an extensive expedition aimed at sweeping the Indians from the region of Texas known as the Llano Estacado, or Staked Plains. A detailed explanation of this campaign follows in the narrative of that regiment's history. During the following ten years, the Tenth Cavalry participated in countless small campaigns against bands of Apache, Lipan, and Kickapoo throughout the region. In 1880, the regiment participated in a major campaign with comrades from the Ninth Cavalry and other units against the Warm Spring Apaches known as the Victorio War.

Following the conclusion of the Victorio War in 1880, unprecedented peace settled over the Texas-Mexico border region. This harmony allowed the Tenth Cavalry to concentrate its companies at Forts Concho, Stockton, and Davis, although the troopers continued to patrol the Rio Grande to the south and the Guadalupe Mountains to the west.

In 1882, Fort Davis became regimental headquarters. For the next three years, the Tenth obtained a welcome rest from the constant campaigning of previous years. As more settlers arrived in west Texas, the region became more subdued and the Tenth Cavalry's Indian fighting experience was no longer required. By early 1885, the regiment assembled to march from the Department of Texas to the Department of Arizona, where those skills would be tested once again.

After arriving in Arizona, various troops of the regiment were dispersed throughout the area to cover as much territory as possible: regimental headquarters and one troop were stationed at Whipple Barracks, five troops at Fort Grant, three at Fort Thomas, two at Fort Verde, and one at Fort Apache. Commanders sent four companies almost immediately from Fort Grant into the field to join the campaign against Geronimo.

Sgt. Armistead engaged in one of the maneuvers a cavalryman had to learn by bringing his horse to ground to serve as cover during combat. *Museum of Natural History Museum, Mesa*

Apache scouts and black troopers teamed up in Arizona Territory at the conclusion of the campaign against Geronimo and his illusive followers. *Steve Turner*

Hauling water when in the field proved no easy task, as these men detailed from Fort Verde, Arizona, from the Tenth United States Cavalry found in the 1880s. *LC*

The regimental colors of the Tenth United States Cavalry (1887–1902) were hand painted on yellow silk. *Anthony Powell*

For months detachments combed the Sierra Madre Mountains in search of Geronimo and his followers. In March 1886, Geronimo agreed to cease fighting but changed his mind and managed to escape quickly. Despite a vigilant month-long chase by the Fourth and Tenth Cavalry regiments, Geronimo slipped across the border into Mexico. The men of the Tenth were withdrawn from the remainder of the campaign and ordered to arrest and transport 400 Chiricahua Apaches— most of whom had remained on the reservation during Geronimo's defiant last stand in September 1886—to Holbrook, Arizona, where they were placed on trains bound for Florida.

In addition, troopers from the Tenth participated in the last fighting of the Apache Wars. One small band of Apaches led by Mangus remained at large; Troop H finally cornered them on September 18, 1886, forcing their surrender. By the time of Mangus' surrender, every troop in the entire Tenth Cavalry had taken part in the closing campaign of the Apache Wars.

In July 1886, the regiment's headquarters moved to Fort Grant, then to Santa Fe later that year. For the next five years, the Tenth Cavalry experienced relative harmony in northwestern New Mexico and parts of Arizona, quelling an occasional outbreak from the nearby reservation. In 1887, elements of the regiment participated in a futile manhunt against the Apache Kid, a former Indian scout turned desperado.

In 1890, the Tenth Cavalry experienced its first change of command when Col. Benjamin Grierson at last received promotion to brigadier general and retired. His successor, Col. J. K. Mizner, would lead the Tenth for seven years until his own promotion to brigadier general. When Col. Mizner took command, he moved regimental headquarters back to Fort Grant. The only other major incident during the Tenth Cavalry's time in the Southwest took place on the Hopi reservation in 1891. The previous year, the United States government began to enforce a compulsory attendance policy at Indian Agency schools. Unrest among the Hopi grew to such heights that in the summer of 1891 two troops of the Tenth Cavalry were dispatched to the reservation to help calm the unrest.

In August 1891, Col. Mizner wrote the adjutant general of the army, requesting that the Tenth Cavalry be relocated. He stressed that the army had stationed the regiment south of the thirty-sixth latitude for more than twenty years. Mizner specifically requested a gradual change of climate, with assignment not farther north than Kansas. Part of this request was ignored because while the Tenth Cavalry was ordered to a new locale, in midwinter it was to be assigned to the icy tundra of Montana. Regimental headquarters went to Fort Custer while troops were dispersed at Forts Assinniboine and Keogh (Montana), Buford (North Dakota), and Leavenworth (Kansas).

In general, the years spent in Montana and North Dakota were a great relief after so long a stint of trying duty in the Southwest. Garrison tasks, hunting parties, and practice marches took up most of the soldiers' time. Sports, including baseball and football, became the preferred recreational pursuits of the soldiers.

Although the campaign against Geronimo had concluded, elements of the Tenth United States Cavalry still continued to be active in Arizona and remained occupied with such assignments as guarding Apache prisoners who were being sent for trial in Tucson. *NARA*

When Gen. Wesley Merritt took an 1894 excursion to the West a detachment from the Tenth United States Cavalry accompanied him. Some of Merritt's party halt for lunch at St. Mary's, Montana. *Montana Historical Society, Helena*

During the early 1890s, when John J. Pershing had this photograph taken, he attempted to transfer from the Tenth United States Cavalry to the quartermaster department, possibly in the belief that he would further his career in doing so. The transfer never took place and by "Black Jack" remaining with the regiment he gained a nickname and very probably rose to greater heights than he would have had he left the unit. *Mark Kasal*

But life was not all play and no work. The Tenth occasionally was called upon to restore civil order or quell unrest off the reservations.

In April 1894, three troops from Fort Custer were dispatched to guard railroad trains belonging to "Coxey's Army," a group of unemployed men on their way to protest in Washington. Other troops were detailed to guard the railroad from strikers later that summer. In the summer of 1896, the entire regiment was in the field rounding up Cree Indians who had fled from their reservations in Canada and dogged them back to their homeland in the north. One of the leaders of this assignment was 1st Lt. John J. Pershing, who in his first duty assignment led Troop D over 600 miles while chasing the Indians. Later known as "Black Jack" Pershing, the future general acquired that nickname from his service with the Tenth Cavalry.

By 1897, the Tenth Cavalry had its second change of command when Col. Mizner gained his star and Col. Guy V. Henry took charge of the unit. That same year, several troops were called out to the Tongue River Indian Agency to resolve a disturbance among the Cheyenne. They made a few arrests and the outbreak died down. At the end of the year, the regiment consolidated at Forts Assinniboine and Keogh, where they remained until the outbreak of the Spanish-American War.

The Infantry

Compared to the cavalry, the infantry led a boring life—no daring chases across the wilderness and no last-minute rescues of supply trains or besieged cavalry companies. While the infantry's function was less visible than the cavalry's, this does not imply that their efforts and accomplishments were less important. The Twenty-fourth and Twenty-fifth Infantry regiments participated in some of the most important military campaigns in the West. The infantry was also instrumental in advancing the settlement of the West, devoting much of their time to standing guard, riding shotgun on mail/passenger stagecoaches, building roads, and stringing telegraph wire.

Some of the story was similar to the horse soldiers, in that the first black foot soldiers were the result of the August 1, 1866, congressional legislation that originally created four African American infantry regiments: the Thirty-eighth, Thirty-ninth, Fortieth, and Forty-first. These regiments served on the frontier and in the Reconstruction South for the next three years, becoming disciplined units.

In late 1866, the Thirty-eighth United States Infantry regiment was organized in St. Louis, Missouri. Early the following year, most of the regiment trudged off to New Mexico, with two companies posted in Kansas to protect railroad workers. In the summer of 1867, one of the companies in Kansas helped defend Fort Wallace against an attack by Cheyenne. The black troops in New Mexico also fought with Indians.

The regimental colors of the Twenty-fourth United States Infantry (1869–1902) were hand painted on blue silk. *Anthony Powell*

In 1881, the Army adopted a European inspired dress helmet with a stylish helmet plate bearing the regimental numeral in German silver, such as this example for an enlisted man in the Twenty-fourth Infantry. Foot soldiers of the Twenty-fifth Infantry were issued the same pattern of plate but with the number "25" affixed to the shield. *Jerome Greene*

The Thirty-ninth United States Infantry was organized in Greenville, Louisiana (near New Orleans), in August 1866. During the next three years it was posted throughout southern Louisiana and western Mississippi. In January 1868, regimental headquarters transferred from Greenville to Ship Island, Mississippi, where it remained for a year. By January 1869, regimental headquarters had returned to Louisiana—first to New Orleans and then to Jackson Barracks.

The Fortieth United States Infantry was organized in Washington, DC, in September 1866. Shortly thereafter, regimental headquarters moved to Camp Distribution, Virginia. During the next two years, the regiment's companies were stationed at sundry posts in North and South Carolina (Forts Macon, Hatteras, Fisher, Caswell, Kinston, Plymouth, and Goldsboro in North Carolina and Castle Pinckney, Walterboro, Orangeburg, and Hilton Head, South Carolina), never staying at one location more than a few months. In 1868, the Army more or less consolidated the regiment in North Carolina, assigning the companies at Goldsboro and Raleigh.

Immediately after its organization, the Forty-first United States Infantry regiment was ordered to posts along the Rio Grande, with regimental headquarters established at Fort McKavett. Unfortunately, little has been written about the Forty-first Infantry, but its successor unit would gain considerable laurels.

This would take place after the regular Army was reduced from forty-five infantry regiments to twenty-five. As a result, the four black regiments were consolidated into two regiments. On April 20, 1869, the Thirty-ninth and Fortieth were reorganized and renumbered as the Twenty-fifth. Seven months later, the Thirty-eighth and Forty-first regiments became the Twenty-fourth Infantry.

The main function of these infantry units on the western frontier continued as support to the cavalry. The infantry was not well suited nor equipped to fight highly mobile American Indians. If the cavalrymen had trouble catching them, the infantry had little or no chance. On occasion infantrymen were mounted and assigned to scouting patrols, but mostly their duties consisted of guard and fatigue details, fort repair, and escort assignments.

An 1886 inspector general's report of Fort Sisseton, Dakota Territory, summed up his observations of elements of the Twenty-fifth Infantry who were posted there. His finding might be taken as representative of black infantrymen at frontier garrisons when he wrote:

> The police of the post was admirable; neatness, order and cleanliness characterized every part of it. The arrangements of the contents of the storehouse, the interiors of the barracks, the grounds surrounding the barracks, quarters, stables and outbuildings; walks, drives, fences, and outlying grounds for two hundred yards in every direction were in perfect order. At 9:00 a.m., Friday Oct 1st, the troops were paraded in full dress uniform for a review, inspection, and drill. The ceremony of review was correctly performed. The "march past" in quick and double time was particularly well done, cadences and alignments well preserved. The subsequent inspection showed the arms, belts, and boxes and the clothing (military dress) to be in excellent order. The appearance of the troops under arms, their carriage and bearing was military in a satisfactory degree. (Nankin 1972, 38)

As indicated, one of the black troops' most frequent assignments was guarding the stage lines' remount stations, on the roads between the forts and frontier towns. Remount station guard duty was generally quiet and a welcome relief from the routine of garrison life. Most of the stages carried mail and freight, but if there were white passengers, stationmasters frequently refused to allow off-duty black infantrymen to board the stage. This discrimination led Col. William Shafter, one of the officers of the Twenty-fourth Infantry, to threaten the stage companies with the removal of the guards if they continued to mistreat his troops. Government supply trains and survey parties also relied on the protection of the infantry. Constructing roads and stringing telegraph lines were duties that often fell to the infantrymen.

This is not to say that the black foot soldiers avoided coming under fire. A number of instances of risking life and limb took place. Arguably the most notable incident was one that could have been a plot from the golden age of Hollywood westerns. It began as routine duty for a joint Twenty-fourth Infantry and Tenth

As one inspector pronounced when reviewing men of the Twenty-fifth Infantry in Dakota Territory, "The appearance of the troops under arms, their carriage and bearing was military in a satisfactory degree." (John H. Nankinvell, *The History of the Twenty-fifth Regiment of Infantry, 1869-1920* [Fort Collins, CO: Old Army Press, 1972], 38) This accolade could have been applied to Cpt. Charles Bentzoni's Company B of the regiment at Fort Randall, with perhaps the exception of the frizzy little terrier who has taken place in front of the double ranks of men in their full dress finery. The first sergeant in the front left near his captain might be wondering: "Whose dog is this?"

James Moss, West Point Class of 1894, was among the pioneer advocates for bicycle infantry. Assigned to Fort Missoula, Montana, with the Twenty-fifth Infantry, 2nd Lt. Moss proposed an experiment. He and enlisted men from his company would venture from the fort to various destinations with full field kits averaging nearly eighty pounds. The first outings were relatively brief, but gradually the range was expanded. In early 1897, Moss sought authority to traverse an impressive distance—nearly 2,000 miles from western Montana to St. Louis, Missouri.

After Moss received a favorable reply, he went on a fact-finding mission to many eastern-based factories, returning with data making it possible for him to design a rugged, two-wheeled vehicle that would hold up to the rigors of the long journey. Along with the subaltern's system of loading gear for each of his command's twenty free-wheeling African American infantrymen, the Fort Missoula cyclists were ready for the rough ride ahead.

Setting out from their post on June 14, 1897, the well-prepared Twenty-fifth Infantry Bicycle Corps pedaled eastward. Despite heat occasionally soaring to over 110 degrees, rain, and other obstacles, "Uncle Sam's Riders" rolled into St. Louis on July 24—a little over five weeks after setting out on their historic journey.

On October 7, 1896, bicyclists from the Twenty-fifth United States Infantry pause at Minerva Terrace, Yellowstone Park, on their arduous overland trek to Missouri. *Haynes Foundation Collection Montana Historical Society, Helena*

Lt. James Moss selected some of the Twenty-fifth United States Infantry regiment's most fit men at Fort Missoula, Montana, to take part in the bicycle experiment he proposed to the War Department. *Haynes Foundation Collection Montana Historical Society, Helena*

In this c. 1880 portrait a Twenty-fourth United States Infantry sergeant displays an old-fashioned brass stadia—an early award to single out expert marksmen. Many black soldiers became noted for their expertise with firearms. *US Army Military History Institute*

Chapter 3
NO PLACE LIKE HOME
Garrison Life

Practice on horseback formed part of the routine for cavalry as indicated by men of the Tenth United
Cavalry, Troop A, posted to Fort Verde, Arizona, from the mid-1880s through early 1890s. *LC*

Troopers of the Tenth United States Cavalry fall out for guard mount at Fort Washakie, Wyoming. This was one of many daily rituals at frontier military posts from the Mississippi River to the Pacific Ocean. *Wyoming State Historical Society*

Although arduous field service from Mexico to Canada forged many of the black regulars into a formidable fighting force, most of their time was spent in and around their garrisons. As was the case for all frontier soldiers, African American troops occupied and maintained outposts that sometimes were isolated and lonely, participating in the full gamut of mundane daily duties that represented a routine seldom broken, except during holidays and under other circumstances.

For instance, the men drilled frequently.

According to John J. Pershing, who had served as an officer with a troop of the Tenth Cavalry during his early military career, they did so to "perfection." Pershing also contended, "The troops required little of the officers. The ranks were filled with veterans and the power and prestige of the old top sergeant was sufficient to maintain sufficient discipline and manage the minor details of administration." Other training might include instruction in the use of pack train equipment that enabled supplies to keep pace with troops on the move in rugged terrain.

Honing other combat skills also consumed many hours. Men would spend time at the target range, or might have to become familiar with new revolvers and other more advanced weapons when they replaced earlier models, as well as achieving familiarity with "machine guns," such as short-barreled and long-barreled Gatling guns or breech-loading Hotchkiss field pieces. In the case of Gatling guns, one officer at Fort Assiniboine, Montana, noted, "The men are unskilled in their use, but men here can be trained to use them in a few hours." One Hotchkiss mountain gun was on hand at that post too, and practice in its use was presumably undertaken. These fast-firing mobile artillery pieces were some of the most up-to-date ordnance in United States Army inventory of the era and just one example that black units, despite unfounded claims in some

A squadron of Tenth United States Cavalry form with their troop trumpeters massed on the right and stand ready for review at Fort Grant, Arizona. Each man is the model of a professional soldier. Behind them appears a small man-made body of water known as Lake Constance, named in honor of the daughter of the squadron commander, Maj. Anson Mills. *NARA*

In the late 1860s, the four infantry regiments manned by black foot soldiers were consolidated into a pair of regiments. An unknown sergeant most likely from the Twenty-fourth Infantry was one of these stalwarts, as indicated by his many "hash marks" on the lower sleeve of his 1874-pattern sack coat he had made a career in the military, with each diagonal stripe indicating five years' service. He is indicative of the top sergeants who kept discipline within their companies in the regiments manned by black soldiers. *Herb Peck Jr.*

histories, usually received issue of armaments, equipment, and mounts for cavalrymen on par with units manned by white personnel.

Be that as it may, besides receiving, becoming familiar with, and maintaining their gear, black troops stood inspection, did their turn at guard mount, and similar martial duties, plus parading. Occasionally they formed for memorial ceremonies for a deceased superior or when laying a comrade to rest.

They also engaged in physical fitness exercises that were coming into vogue during the late Victorian era. Additionally, black soldiers participated in organized athletic competitions, including baseball and track and field events. The latter activities might be mentioned in newspapers such as in Utah like the *Broad Ax*, *Plain Dealer*, and some Salt Lake area periodicals that carried stories of sporting events held by the Twenty-fourth Infantry and on occasion favorably mentioned the regiment's "crack drilling" and band.

Attendance at a garrison school was sometimes required for several soldiers as well. Indeed, many of the enlisted men (either black or white) had little or no formal education when they entered the military of the era. To overcome this deficiency the army established post schools—albeit separate ones for black and white soldiers, one of the many examples of the official segregation policy existing at the time. These schools operated under the watchful eye of the garrison or regimental chaplain, a practice that continued through the mid-1890s, and even beyond in some instances. In most cases, while actually not engaged in teaching the troops, the chaplains performed in a supervisory capacity. Usually enlisted personnel turned educators instructed both their fellow soldiers and the children of the garrison, although a civilian was periodically hired to take on the latter task.

More strenuous physical chores than learning the three "R"s were part of the regimen too, from cutting ice, securing wood for lumber and fuel, working at numerous non-military tasks known as fatigues, construction of post facilities, tending post gardens, and working in the mess hall or company kitchen on "KP."

At times military prisoners undertook such chores. More frequently enlisted men were assigned or placed on special details or extra duty, requirements that sometimes took soldiers away from their martial schedule, much to the chagrin of their commanders. Their tasks ranged from reporting to the quartermaster as teamsters or day laborers to undertaking other assignments, such as work in the post library, serving as a janitor in the post exchange, performing as carpenters, logging operations to obtain fuel and building materials, or picking wild berries near the fort as a supplemental food source. Additionally they might take on the responsibility of working for an officer for extra pay as a "striker," handling a variety of tasks from cleaning boots to household jobs. These "dog robbers" not only received extra income from the officer who engaged them, but also might benefit from this position on occasion, including bunking in a spare room of the officer's quarters rather than having to live in a communal open bay barracks where privacy was impossible.

Troop A, Tenth United States Cavalry at parade rest at Fort Apache, Arizona, during March 1887, demonstrate that troopers were also required to master dismounted drill as well as drill on horseback. *University of Arizona Library, Special Collections*

By 1892, Troop A, Tenth United Cavalry had transferred to Fort Keogh, Montana, where saber practice remained part of the regimen even if the weapon had limited application in combat by the late Victorian era. *Casey Bathelmess Family*

A Tenth United States Cavalry trumpeter sounds a call at Fort Keogh, Montana, in the 1890s. The bugle governed the day for soldiers in the West. *Casey Barthelmess Family*

Other athletic events, such as tug of war, helped pass time and keep soldiers fit in garrison. *US Army Military History Institute*

83

The contention by some authors that blacks troops received inferior equipment and mounts had little basis in reality. For instance, in 1892, members of Company F, Twenty-fourth United States Infantry posted to Fort Bayard, New Mexico, were provided with cutting edge experimental blanket roll field equipment designed by 1st Lt. Charles Dodge Jr. for trial. *NARA*

Taking a break from martial routine, men of the Ninth United States Cavalry at Fort Bayard, New Mexico, play a game of the national sport—baseball—that grew ever more popular in the post-Civil War. *US Army Military History Institute*

Many black and white soldiers lacked education. The Army provided schooling, in this case under direction of the post chaplain for Fort Keogh, Montana, I. Newton Ritner. *Christian Barthelmess Family*.

Driving the water wagon from the nearby river also required troopers to be detailed for extra duty at Fort Verde, Arizona. *LC*

Numerous non-military tasks required troop labor, including cutting ice for the post icehouse, as these infantrymen do to help preserve food for Fort Keogh, Montana's, garrison. *US Army Military History Institute*

Not all the black soldier's time was spent in garrison. They frequented the nearby target range, while maneuvers increasingly took troops to the field, with considerable emphasis being placed on war games and practice marches in the later 1800s and early 1900s.

Further, the men escorted paymasters and high-ranking officers from post to post. But it was not all work and no play. Hunting and fishing afforded leisure and supplemented the often bland, unvaried rations issued by the Army.

Paydays and other off-duty time allowed troops to leave the post for nearby civilian communities and entities, not all of which were well received by military superiors. As an example, an article in the October 24, 1896, issue of the Salt Lake *Broad Ax* reported the Twenty-fourth Infantry's chaplain would have been "more pleased if all the saloons, gambling houses and immoral houses" of Salt Lake "would absolutely refuse negro soldiers" because he believed there were "a thousand white men who are willing to go to hell with the black man, but there are very few willing to go to heaven with him."

Of course, there were more socially acceptable amusements, such as "Hops" (military slang for dances). As Elijah Cox—an old timer and fiddle player of the Twenty-fifth Infantry—reminisced in a 1924 newspaper interview:

"There wasn't none of them turkey trots in that day," said the old fiddler. "Folks danced the schottische, the polka, the square dance, and the quadrille. We had real music in them days, too. I'll bet I can play 300 waltzes, all of them different without stopping." (*Standard*, May 3, 1924)

The spouse of the post surgeon at Fort Concho, Texas, Mrs. James W. Buell, took a different point of view. She recorded:

We went to a little dance Friday evening at General Grierson's and I nearly killed myself laughing. It was a regular frontier dance with the most absurd old negro to call off the most ridiculous quadrilles, and every one danced in true negro style. (Miles 1960, 42)

Alice Grierson would not have agreed with this opinion. She noted a "fancy dress ball" held in February 1876 was quite a fine affair. Later she lamented the loss of Fort Concho's accomplished string band due to the death of one of its members and the hospitalization of a second key performer.

Women with whom to trip the light fantastic might be another matter. When elements of the Ninth Cavalry rode into Fort Wingate, New Mexico, in January 1876 originally, as the post surgeon scribbled in his diary, there were "no Desdemonas with these Othellos." By August that situation had changed, as the same diarist indicated: "The men of the colored companies have a hop this night…. We have had quite an accession of colored females with the recently arrived cavalry, and I hear there will be no lack of partners." (Utley 2014, 90)

To maintain their married status soldiers might have to make extra funds by taking on outside work, as this Tenth Cavalry trooper and his spouse evidently have done at Fort Verde, Arizona, where they performed various duties for an officer's family. *LC*

Serving as a guardian to children also might fall to a soldier as extra duty, hopefully for a stipend, especially if the offspring of officers were unruly. *NARA*

Pvt. Freeman of the Twenty-fifth United States Infantry band evidently served as a "striker" for regimental adjutant 1st Lt. George Andrews, seen here at Fort Snelling, Minnesota. If Freeman indeed served as an extra duty helper to the lieutenant, among other things he could have taken care of Andrews' horse "Old Bob," whom the officer pronounced "the best horse ever," and Dash, who was "a fine retriever." *Mark Kasal*

As Rudyard Kipling quipped, "single men in barracks don't grow into plaster saints," but the black soldier, despite his Spartan surroundings, found life at a frontier fort more desirable than the Jim Crow world that existed outside the post. This representative example of the open style barracks that most enlisted troops called home in the West was at Fort Huachuca, Arizona. *NARA*

When not engaged in field operations, frontier soldiers spent time at the range for target practice, as they do here at Fort Bayard, New Mexico Territory. *US Army Military History Institute*

Some soldiers were fortunate enough to marry and enjoy families, although doing so was not easy in the frontier army, where it seemed the concept was if the Army wanted an enlisted man to have a wife they would have issued him one. *Anthony Powell*

Regimental musician Sgt. Bannister and his family were in the minority, as most soldiers were single. *Anthony Powell*

Leona Howard Allen gracefully poses in her finest, befitting the wife of senior non-commissioned officer Sgt. David Allen of the Ninth United States Cavalry. *Anthony Powell*

95

During most of the first quarter century of existence for regiments manned by black soldiers, the troops served south of the Mason-Dixon Line. By 1888, Company I, Twenty-fifth United Infantry would be one of the companies sent north to Fort Snelling, Minnesota. *NARA*

The band and a company of the Twenty-fifth United States Infantry smartly turn out at Fort Randall, Dakota Territory, in 1880. Military pomp and daily "housekeeping" chores alternated the everyday life of a black frontier regular. *NARA*

common [for black troops] than in the rest of the Army." The stimulus varied for this, sometimes being reminiscent of life under the "peculiar institution." By way of example:

> The son of a frontier officer recalled one instance when an entire Twenty-fifth Infantry company harmonized on a series of melancholy spirituals, subsequent to the unit's being confined to quarters by an exasperated officer. After listening to the melodious laments, the officer relented and lifted the restriction." (Rickey 1963, 188–89)

Music, then, could be used to communicate anguish, discontent, or other emotions.

Bands

One manifestation of unit pride could be found in the excellent bands that formed part of the black regiments. The Tenth Cavalry proved particularly noteworthy because Grierson—a former schoolteacher and accomplished musician in his own right—sought perfection for his bandsmen. The colonel called for men who could read and write (no mean accomplishments in a time when literacy rates were far from high), as well as individuals who demonstrated a capability for learning music. James H. Thomas, who enlisted in 1867, did not disappoint his commander's expectations when he assumed the position of chief musician. He held this post for three decades, leading the regimental players to the peak of perfection.

The Twenty-fifth infantry's band deserved similar accolades. For instance, during the summer of 1883, an invitation came from Minneapolis' Shattuck Military School for the musicians to perform. The commandant of the school reported, "The band proved to be all that we had expected from the reports, which had reached us before we heard them...." The same observer pronounced these bandsmen were, "Skilled in the use of their instruments, and orderly in their deportment." (Powell 1994, 4)

On September 13, 1883, the regimental musicians from the Twenty-fifth Infantry repeated their success, pleasing crowds at the Minnesota State Fair. Five years later they enlivened the Memorial Day parade in a Montana community where one observer contended they, "discoursed the sweetest music ever heard in Missoula." In addition to parade appearances, the band offered regular concerts in town on Thursday evening, thereby cementing good relations between the civilian population and the personnel of the regiment. They even played at the funeral of a prominent Missoula citizen in October 1889.

Mounted on white horses, the band of the Tenth United States Cavalry leads a mounted parade at Fort Custer, Montana. *US Army Military History Institute*

The Twenty-fifth United States Infantry band was popular at Fort Missoula, Montana, during their posting at that garrison in the 1890s. *University of Montana Mansfield Library*

Posing in a picturesque bandstand in 1896, the Twenty-fourth United States Infantry regimental musicians played for fellow soldiers and local Salt Lake City, Utah, residents alike. *Anthony Powell*

Kentuckian James W. Abbott was born in 1860. He rapidly rose through the ranks after his enlistment in 1881 with the Twenty-fourth United States Infantry at Fort Douglas, Utah. Abbott became the regimental sergeant major and in 1897 was appointed a post ordnance sergeant, one of the top positions as a member of the non-commissioned staff that provided an opportunity for higher pay and separate quarters outside the barracks. He had this portrait taken soon after his promotion when he was stationed at Fort Bayard, New Mexico. *George M. Langellier Jr.*

Chapter 4
THEY LOOK LIKE MEN
Enlisted Ranks

William H. Brice, shown here as a
quartermaster sergeant with Company
D, Twenty-fourth United States Infantry,
enlisted in 1888 and spent twenty-six
years with the regiment, including in the
Philippines. *Anthony Powell*

When commander of the Ninth United States Cavalry Col. Edward Hatch died in 1889, the senior enlisted men of the regiment were on hand for his funeral at Fort Robinson, Nebraska. They were (back row, left to right): 1st Sgt. George Wilson; 1st Sgt. David Badie; 1st Sgt. Thomas Shaw; and Sgt. Nathan Fletcher. Front row (left to right): chief trumpeter Stephen Taylor; Sgt. Edmund McKinzie; Sgt. Robert Burley; and Sgt. Zekiel Sykes. *United States Military Academy Library*

In the wake of the Civil War, the West offered perceived opportunities for nearly every element of society. So it was that some blacks banded together in groups to cross the Mississippi River as "exodusters" bent on establishing a new society in the heartland of Kansas. Other blacks came as individuals to farm, establish businesses, or engage in various livelihoods, including the profession of arms.

Indeed, a number of blacks—many of whom were previously enslaved—joined the Army as a potential avenue to advancement, adventure, and even escape from an old way of life, such as from prosecution by the law, marital issues, and unemployment. For some would-be soldiers a psychological element many have come into play. Supposedly:

> Black military organizations projected images that met their members' deepest needs. Prestige, dress, and bearing, of course varied with rank and insignia, but all men in uniform were differentiated from the anonymous souls that walked the streets in ordinary garments, in search of themselves and companionship. (Daniels 1980, 133)

There was also the possibility that the Army provided a means to economic or social betterment. This included educational opportunities for some knowledge-thirsty men who viewed formal learning as a road worth traveling, particularly after the Freedmen's Bureau ceased to exist. For instance, George Conrad Jr. stated that when he entered the Ninth United States Cavalry he was illiterate, but like his father whom "the white folks learned…how to read and write," he would acquire the same skills once he had entered service. (Dobak and Phillips, *Black Regulars*, 47)

Additionally, individuals who had been displaced by the Civil War could find food, shelter, clothing, and medical benefits by entering the military. The last factor prompted Joshua Johnson to become a trooper with the Tenth United States Cavalry. He developed hemorrhoids during his service in the Union Army but did not have the money to pay a physician. Thus, the perfunctory physical examine by the military that he received prior to signing on allowed him to hide his preexisting condition so that a military doctor would have to treat him after he reported for duty.

Born in Platte City, Missouri, Benjamin Brown listed his occupation as a packer when he enlisted at twenty-five at Fort Leavenworth, Kansas, in 1881. Reporting to the Twenty-fourth United States Infantry, Brown became a "lifer" as an infantryman, a crack shot, regimental band member, and recipient of the Medal of Honor for his valor during the robbery of the army payroll bound from Forts Grant to Thomas, Arizona, in 1889. *Anthony Powell*

Alabaman Paschal Conley was born in January 1859. Conley enlisted in 1879 and served until 1906, including with the Tenth Cavalry in Cuba. Lt. John Pershing recommended Conley for a commission as "a fitting recognition of long and honorable service," but 110 years passed before the United States Congress acted favorably on the recommendation. *Anthony Powell*

One way for enlisted men to attain upward mobility was to take an exam for a staff non-commissioned officer, which included quartermaster sergeants. Men such as Pennsylvanian Benjamin F. Davis, an original member of Troop M, Tenth United States Cavalry, was one of those ambitious men who passed the examination to become a quartermaster sergeant in 1885. A decade later he retired at Fort Robinson, Nebraska, with a reception and banquet acknowledging his nineteen years as the Tenth's regimental sergeant major and later as a post quartermaster sergeant. *Denver Public Library*

Some even volunteered to demonstrate they were free to pursue any course they wished, rather than be restrained by their old lifestyle, which was often forced on them. Then, too, certain veterans who had served in the Union forces—and others inspired by the record compiled during the Civil War— evidently thought their experiences as soldiers were worth continuing. Indeed, as the *Black Regulars* indicates, "About half of the black men who joined the regular army in the late 1860s had served during the Civil War." Statistics of the enlistees who joined the black regiments in 1866 bear this assertion, given that out of approximately 2,100 men who signed on in that year 562 listed their former occupation as soldier or discharged soldier. (See Table 1)

Occupations Listed by Black US Army Enlistees, 1866

Baker 2	Drummer 2	Plasterer 1
Barber 26	Engineer 1	Porter 1
Barkeeper 1	Farmer 487	Poston Railer 1
Blacksmith 18	Farrier 1	Oiler 2
Boatman/	Fireman 2	Ostler 2
Steam Boatman 55	Fuller 1	Riverman 11
Bookkeeper 1	Furman 2	Sailor/Mariner 44
Bricklayer/Brick Mason 6	Gardner 1	Servant 31
Brick Maker 1	Groom 1	Shoemaker 9
Brick Moulder 1	Hackman 1	Slater 3
Bugler 3	Herder 5	Soldier/
Butcher 3	Hostler 16	Discharged Soldier 562
Butler 1	Iron Worker 1	Spinner 2
Cattle Driver 1	Joiner 1	Steward 5
Carpenter 16	Kettle Sitter 1	Stockman 1
Cart Man 1	Laborer 589	Sugarman 1
Cigar Maker 2	Machinist 2	Tanner 2
Clerk 3	Mason 3	Teamster 21
Coachman 5	Mattress Maker 1	Tinner 1
Coalman 1	Mechanic 1	Tobacco Stemmer 1
Cook 28	Merchant 1	Wagoner 6
Cooper 1	Miller 5	Waiter 64
Confectioner 1	Musician 9	Table 2
Dentist 1	Painter 7	
Distiller 1	Paperhanger 1	

HUISH BROS.   PHOTOGRAPHERS, PAYSON, UTAH.

Dapper Pvt. Charles Drayton strums a guitar at the photographer's studio.
Anthony Powell

While serving at Fort Buford, North Dakota, Pvt. Carter Huse of the Twenty-fifth United States Infantry completed four five-year enlistments, as indicated by the gold lace chevrons on his lower sleeves. In a great number of cases black soldiers had a high rate of reenlistment, staying with the military until retirement and often completing thirty or more years on duty. *State Historical Society of North Dakota*

Born in Charles County, Maryland, just a few months after the outbreak of the Civil War, 5'7"
Jeremiah Jones would enlist in the Ninth Cavalry at twenty. He moved up the ranks from private to
sergeant major during the next quarter of a century, then passed the examination for post
ordnance sergeant. Jones received his appointment in 1897 to this desirable posting and served at
Forts Whipple and Huachuca in Arizona, Jefferson Barracks, Missouri, and Fort Logan, Colorado,
where he died from pneumonia on March 20, 1906, leaving a widow, the former Annie L. Brown.
Museum of the Non-Commissioned Officer, United States Army

From Carter's Ridge, Virginia, Isaiah Mays of the Twenty-fourth United States Infantry was also one of the escorts for Maj. Joseph W. Wham and the Army payroll made off with by a gang of robbers in a well-planned ambush in Arizona. Mays would receive the Medal of Honor, but after his death on May 2, 1925, he was buried in Phoenix, Arizona, in a pauper's grave until reinterred decades later with the dignity he deserved in Arlington National Cemetery. *LC*

reorganization and downsizing of the Army, he would become a fixture of the Twenty-fourth United States Infantry. During the Spanish-American War he temporarily left the Twenty-Fourth to accept a commission with the black Ninth Infantry, United States Volunteers, but not before receiving a second combat wound, this time at San Juan Hill.

Hector Preston's company commander invited his subordinate to reenlist after expiration with the United States Colored Troops (USCT). Preston replied he would do so "after he had rested awhile." It behooved him not to wait too long because those who rejoined more than thirty days after departing service lost the $1 a month bonus their previous term of enlistment permitted. This proved the case for nearly 2,500 USCT veterans who delayed signing on again in the allotted period.

Robert Anderson's stretch with the 125th US Colored Infantry also numbered him among the Civil War survivors who continued to wear Uncle Sam's blue after the clash ended between the North and South. In his autobiography *From Slavery to Affluence* Anderson recorded: "My company was ordered to Kansas, and became part of the army that corralled the Indians on the reservation in what was known as Indian Territory," where he and his comrades in arms trudged across country afoot, but not without incident. About a month after Anderson and his unit marched from Missouri toward Texas, a raiding party crossed their path. Anderson's account of the encounter read like a Hollywood plot: "We expected a battle, and the [supply] wagons were all drawn in a circle, and the horse and mules staked inside the circle, and the regiment drawn up in battle formation." Thinking better of striking the Indians did not attack, but the infantrymen remained in their makeshift bastion that night; as Anderson confessed, "none of us slept much."

Another black Civil War soldier, George Washington Williams claimed to have run away from Bedford Springs, Pennsylvania, to take up soldiering. The fourteen-year-old son of free blacks never knew the sting of an overseer's lash, but he was intent on striking a blow against the Confederacy. To do so, he must have given a false age to the recruiter, which likewise may account for his apparent use of an assumed name when he entered Company C, Forty-first US Colored Troops. This subterfuge worked. The underage impostor soon discovered that his decision was a serious one, because he sustained a wound during September 1864 in the assault against Fort Harris, Virginia. Becoming a casualty did not stop him from a quick return to the front, which threw him back into the thick of combat at "Hatcher's Run, Five Forks and at various points along the sixteen-mile battle line to Petersburg" where some of the final fierce fighting of the war raged.

Surviving shot and shell, after the war Williams took a "few months at home with books," but the brief respite wore thin. He longed "for the outdoors, lively exhilarating exercise of military life." Leaving his home in Newcastle, Williams reached Pittsburg [sic], where on August 29, 1867, he signed on for five years with the Tenth Cavalry. Once he reported to Carlisle Barracks, Pennsylvania, he

Trooper Sancho Mazique enlisted in the Tenth United States Cavalry in 1875 to serve a five year term of enlistment. While with Troop E, Tenth Cavalry he regularly plied his skills as a carpenter. Mazique may have learned this trade while enslaved in his native South Carolina. He died at the ripe old age of 101 in San Angelo, Texas. *Anthony Powell*

Thomas E. Polk was a veteran of the Indian Wars and Philippine Insurrection. He vagabonded in the Ninth United States Cavalry at such posts as Forts Robinson, Nebraska, and D.A. Russell (now F.E. Warren Air Force Base), Wyoming. Polk died on June 24, 1940, in Eden, Maryland. *Anthony Powell*

Cpt. John Bigelow described Tennessee born Alfred M. Ray as a "tall, fine-looking cavalryman." A day after his sixteenth birthday (May 17, 1872) he enlisted as a private in Troop F, Tenth United States Cavalry. Over the next quarter of a century he would serve variously as a saddler, sergeant, first sergeant, and regimental color sergeant, a position of high regard for an especially respected non-commissioned officer. During the Spanish-American War and Philippine Insurrection he held commissions as a first lieutenant first in the Tenth Volunteer Infantry and later in the Forty-ninth Volunteer Infantry. *Anthony Powell*

Born in Fredericksburg, Virginia, John Sample spent two years as an infantryman with the 108th United State Colored Troops. After the Civil War he reenlisted as one of the original soldiers in the Fortieth United States Infantry and remained with the army after the reorganization of infantry regiments, seeing duty with both the Twenty-fourth and Twenty-fifth United States Infantry regiments in Texas and Oklahoma. He became the Twenty-fourth's sergeant major on May 1, 1884. *Anthony Powell*

served as a drill sergeant, instructing fellow recruits before being dispatched to Fort Riley, Kansas, where Col. Grierson relocated regimental headquarters. Once there, at eighteen the callow youth was promoted to the highest enlisted rank and would sport the chevrons of the regiment's sergeant major. In his new position, Williams conceded his days "would flow merrily away at headquarters, with but little to do, far away from the Indian's deadly arrow."

After the regiment concluded its final organization Williams departed with a squadron to garrison Fort Arbuckle, Indian Territory. For the most part the three companies spent much of their time rebuilding the post. This tedious duty meant Williams and his fellow troopers lived in relative safety, yet somehow on May 19, 1868, a bullet ended up in "the interior lobe of the left lung." It is unknown how Williams was wounded. After a period of hospitalization he received a certificate of disability for a wound received "*not in the line of duty* rendering him unfit to perform the duties of a soldier." Consequently, on September 4, 1868, his military career ended prematurely with a dishonorable discharge. A civilian once more, the nineteen-year-old Williams would go on to become a distinguished Baptist minister, the author of the first book treating the history of blacks in the United States, elected as an Ohio state legislator, and worked as a respected newspaper columnist. (Franklin 1985)

While Williams was exceptional in significant ways, he represented many youths in their middle teens accepted during the war to fill quotas assigned for USCT regiments. This meant "… many veterans with one or two years' war service had barely turned eighteen when they applied to regular army recruiters." Consequently, many "minors found their way into the black regiments." (Dobak 2001, 23)

Not all the enlisted men who joined the black regulars were Union volunteers. Madison Bruin was underage during the war, but had observed both Northern and Southern troops in his home state of Kentucky. He recollected: "What did I think when I seed al them sojers? I wants to be one too…wants a gun and a hoss and be a sojer." (Dobak 2001, 21)

Another individual who had lived through the bitter war years but had not fought may well be one of the most unusual recruits to join the regular Army in 1866. Having claimed service as a cook, this Missouri native was born of a freeman father and enslaved mother "belonging to William Johnson, a wealthy farmer…." Her name was Cathy Williams, and according to an account she gave to a reporter many decades later, "The regiment I joined wore the Zouave uniform and only two persons, a cousin and a particular friend, members of the regiment, knew that I was a woman. They never 'blowed' on me."

After peace returned to the land, Williams' wartime experience was "partly the cause of" her desire to join the Army. She also stated, "Another reason was I wanted to make my own living and not be dependent on relations or friends." Induced by these twin motivations, she posed as a man under the assumed name William Cathey. Evidently the physical examine was perfunctory, because she

Cpl. Edward Scott had over eight years of service with the Tenth United States Cavalry when at age thirty he was severely wounded on May 3, 1886, in a fire fight with Apaches in Mexico as a member of Troop K. This action cost him both legs and admission to the Soldiers Home in Washington, DC, where he was admitted for medical disability. *Armed Forces Institute of Pathology*

Thomas Shaw's enlistment in the Ninth United States Cavalry would take the recruit far from his hometown of Covington, Kentucky. While a sergeant with Troop K his heroics against Nana's Apaches at Carrizo Canyon, New Mexico, during the summer of 1881 resulted in a Medal of Honor. *LC*

In 1869 E.D. Gibson started his years of duty with the Tenth United States Cavalry. He "saw many hard fights with the Indians" with the regiment before transferring to the Twenty-fourth Infantry in 1880. He was with that unit in San Carlos, Arizona, and elsewhere, as well as writing a brief history of the regiment in Cuba. *Frontier Army Museum, Fort Leavenworth, Kansas*

Ninth United States Cavalry chief trumpeter Stephen Taylor played the E-flat cornet. He retired in April 1898, just prior to the regiment's departure for Cuba to fight the Spanish. *Anthony Powell*

Ruben Waller once served a Confederate general during the Civil War, but in 1867, as a free man he signed on with the Tenth United States Cavalry at Fort Leavenworth, Kansas. After a few months of drill and equitation "training" Waller rode west to Fort Hays, Kansas, in Troop H under the command of Cpt. Louis H. Carpenter. He saw action including with the relief party that ended the siege at Beecher's Island. *Anthony Powell*

After a few months as a trooper and post librarian with Troop A, Ninth United States Cavalry at Fort Robinson, Nebraska, Vance H. Marchbanks transferred to the Hospital Corps. His time in uniform brought him to such assignments as Fort Washakie, Wyoming, in the north to Fort Huachuca, Arizona, in the Southwest. During World War I he was commissioned a captain and sent to Fort Des Moines, Iowa to help train black officer candidates. *Anthony Powell*

Soldiers, 164) The white bullies did not savor their high-handed bravado for long, because some of Goldsby's comrades went back to the saloon in town where this humiliating incident took place. With weapons in hand, the revenge-seeking soldiers opened fire, killing one of the whites inside and wounding two more. As the smoke cleared, Pvt. John L. Brown was also dead, while one of his comrades was wounded.

Fearing the consequences, Goldsby bolted and disappeared in the vast stretches of the West. On the other hand, when Sgt. Goldsby's youngest son Crawford grew up his fate became part of Western lore. Goldsby's offspring was destined to become the daring, legendary *pistolero* known as "Cherokee Bill."

Goldsby's going over the hill ultimately proved an anomaly, especially when the black regiments settled into their routine within a few years after being raised. For example, by 1876, incidents of desertion for the Ninth Cavalry dropped to only six deserters and in the Tenth Cavalry the number was eighteen. In contrast, during the same year 170, 224, 172, and 174 men fled from the Third, Fifth, Seventh, and Eighth United States Cavalry regiments, respectively. By the next fiscal year (from July 1, 1876, through June 30, 1877) the Ninth and Tenth again ranked lowest among cavalry regiments in numbers of deserters, with the same holding true with the Twenty-fourth and Twenty-fifth Infantry (see Table 3).

For 1885–1886, another government report once more pointed to the dependability of African American troops. This document indicated that during a twelve-month period only three men of the Twenty-fourth US Infantry deserted, in contrast to 104 white enlisted men of the Third United States Cavalry and ninety-nine from the Fifth United States Cavalry. Indeed, the Twenty-fourth Infantry boasted the lowest desertion rate in the entire army from 1880 through 1886, while in 1888, it shared this distinction with the Twenty-fifth Infantry.

Statement showing number of desertions from the United States Army during fiscal year ending June 30, 1877

(Annual Report of the Secretary of War, 1877, 49)			
Engineers	8	Ninth Infantry	59
Ordnance	7	Tenth Infantry	22
First Cavalry	90	Eleventh Infantry	30
Second Cavalry	167	Twelfth Infantry	11
Third Cavalry	170	Thirteenth Infantry	24
Fourth Cavalry	184	Fourteenth Infantry	45
Fifth Cavalry	224	Fifteenth Infantry	30
Sixth Cavalry	.71	Sixteenth Infantry	70
Seventh Cavalry	172	Seventeenth Infantry	27
Eighth Cavalry	174	Eighteenth Infantry	37
Ninth Cavalry	6	Nineteenth Infantry	24
Tenth Cavalry	18	Twentieth Infantry	22
First Artillery	48	Twenty-first Infantry	19
Second Artillery	49	Twenty-second Infantry	22
Third Artillery	33	Twenty-third Infantry	42
Fourth Artillery	41	Twenty-fourth Infantry	7
Fifth Artillery	33	Twenty-fifth Infantry	9
First Infantry	14	Signal service	2
Second Infantry	23	General service, infantry 83	
Third Infantry	46	General service, mounted 147	
Fourth Infantry	86	West Point detachment	10
Fifth Infantry	18	Ft Leavenworth detachment 3	
Sixth Infantry	11	General non-commissioned staff	
Seventh Infantry	45	U.S Army	3
Eighth Infantry	30		
			TOTAL 2,516

What prompted this loyalty? Could it be that potential deserters feared the consequences of their actions more than their white counterparts because the civilian population would be less likely to harbor them? More to the point, it would prove difficult for African Americans to meld into the predominantly white West while making good a break from the military, although there were exceptions to the rule in places like Las Vegas, New Mexico.

These factors may have come into play, but possibly a sense of group identification provided a strong reason for remaining with one's comrades. Another explanation might be the reality, "That life in the military — hard as though it was — was more desirable than life in the civilian population, where racial prejudice and discrimination were harsher...." (Billington 1991, 173)

Brent Woods—another Kentuckian—found a home in the Ninth United States Cavalry. He also campaigned in 1881 against Apaches in New Mexico, performing gallantly. Some thirteen years later, his bravery finally resulted in a long overdue presentation of a Medal of Honor at a ceremony on the parade ground of Fort McKinney, Wyoming, with praise from his commanding officer, "All who know you said that this medal has been worthily bestowed...." *LC*

Other reasons existed for loyalty and for why African Americans troops sustained a high level of morale and *esprit* based upon unit cohesiveness. One historian studying the black infantry opined there seemed to exist: "a strong desire among the men to prove to the army, to society, and to themselves that they could soldier as well as white troops." (Fowler 1971, 79) Also, warrior traditions carried from Africa may have prompted some to take pride in their chosen occupation. Yet, a chaplain serving in a black regiment may have captured the motivations most succinctly. In *Army and Navy Journal* (January 14, 1877) he maintained black enlisted personnel "are possessed of the notion that the colored people of the whole country are more or less affected by the conduct of the Army."

Seminole Negro Scouts

These black scouts were descendants of runaways who fled enslavement by whites and sought refuge in Florida in the late eighteenth and early nineteenth centuries. During the Second Seminole War (1835–1842) they united with the Indians in opposition to American expansion into the region that subsequently led to a bloody, expensive war. Despite desperate fighting, a majority of the Seminoles and blacks were forced to relocate to today's Oklahoma.

In 1849–1850, following their joint removal, blacks led by John Horse and Seminoles under Wild Cat emigrated to Mexico. Nearly a decade later, the Seminoles returned to the United States, but the blacks remained on the Mexican side of the border, where slavery was banned. Some of them even fought against Maximillian's foreign forces and John Horse rose to become a colonel in Benito Juárez's forces.

By 1870, many of the blacks had made their way back to Indian Territory, where they began to be recruited as scouts by United States Army officers. Their knowledge of the wilds of west Texas made these so-called "Seminole Negro-Indian Scouts" invaluable. They served with distinction from 1873 through 1882, engaging in twenty-six expeditions—a dozen of which were major campaigns—and though often heavily outnumbered had not a single man killed or seriously wounded during this intense period. Although they never fielded more than fifty men, their commanders praised them as "excellent hunters and trailers, and splendid fighters," as evidenced by the fact that in spite of their small numbers they would receive an unprecedented four Medals of Honor. Even after warfare with the Comanche and Kiowa concluded, these scouts remained on active duty and continued to serve as long service veteran John July did as a sort of "Avant Courier," as army surgeon John Vance Lauderdale indicated in his diary while stationed at Fort Davis, Texas. Indeed, a small group of this hardy band remained on duty through the early twentieth century at Fort Clark, Texas, where their descendants live to this day.

John Jefferson began his days with the Army as a Seminole Negro scout before joining the Army as a trumpeter with the Tenth United States Cavalry in the 1890s. *Institute of Texan Cultures, San Antonio*

From their base at Fort Clark, Seminole scouts made their mark in Texas as fierce fighters and tireless trackers. *Anthony Powell*

Cadet Johnson Chesnutt Whittaker was one of a dozen blacks admitted to the United States Military Academy in the post-Civil War era. He never completed his studies; a court martial based on charges and a guilty verdict that were both suspect resulted in his dismissal from West Point. *Anthony Powell*

Chapter 5

CADET GRAY & ARMY BLUE

West Point and Officers

Cadet Henry O. Flipper graduated in the Class of 1877 as the first African American to earn his commission from West Point. *United States Military Academy Library*

After surviving four silent years at West Point, Henry O. Flipper became a 2nd lieutenant in the Tenth United States Cavalry. *Pahaska Books*

By 1850, John Hanks Alexander's father purchased the freedom of his enslaved wife and three of their seven children. His parents' efforts to provide a better life for their family bore fruit: Hanks became the second black graduate of West Point, receiving his commission in 1887. *United States Military Academy Library*

The third black graduate of West Point, Charles Young (Class of 1889) was the last African American to receive an appointment to the Academy until Benjamin O. Davis Jr. became a "pleb" in the 1930s. *United States Military Academy Library*

Lt. Alexander later completed other assignments with the Ninth United States Cavalry, which he served "with efficiency and credit until February 1894." At that time the war department detailed him as professor of military science and tactics at Wilberforce University. Scarcely a month later Alexander died "from the rupture of one of the large arteries near the heart." As one obituary noted, Alexander was, "A young man of usual brilliancy, with a long and useful career before him, to be cut down just at the beginning of life, as it were, is a sad blow...." (*Association of Graduates* 1894, 73)

The third and last black graduate of West Point in the nineteenth century enjoyed a much longer career. A native of Helena, Kentucky, following the Civil War's conclusion, Charles Young moved with his parents to the North. Young proved a diligent student. After completing high school, he briefly served as a teacher in his adopted hometown of Ripley, Ohio. During this period Young considered applying for admission to a Jesuit college, but the opportunity arose for him to take the competitive examination for West Point. Young passed the test. In 1884, he was instructed to join his class at West Point.

Young joined other cadets in equitation and cavalry drill as part of the training he received before entering the United States cavalry as a 2nd lieutenant. *United States Military Academy Library*

Young at a West Point dress formation appeared in the rear rank, a highly symbolic position given his second class treatment as a cadet. *United States Military Academy Library*

One of his fellow West Pointers remembered Young in his cadet days as: "... a rather awkward, overgrown lad, large-boned and robust in physique, and of a nervous impulsive temperament." Life at the Academy was lonely because Alexander's graduation and the discharge of other black cadets for low grades left Young the lone black in the cadet corps. With no comrades he seemed, "impelled to talk with anyone who would take an interest in his conversation." This led him to engage in an uncharacteristic activity: exchanges with German-born boot blacks at the Academy in their native language to communicate with another human beyond official exchanges. In this instance, Young's "good working knowledge of Latin, Greek, French, Spanish, and German" paid practical dividends.

During these first years of isolation Young had few occasions to break through the racial wall erected around him by his fellow cadets. Nevertheless, he persevered. Gradually, one West Pointer contended, "his class began to acknowledge and respect his finer traits of character; while a spirit of fair play induced many cadets ... to treat Young with the kindness and consideration long his due." (Rhodes 1922, 152)

For a short period he was sent to Fort Duchesne, Utah; part of his tour overlapped with that of John Alexander. This rare opportunity may have provided some moments for the two men to share a comradeship they had been denied in the white-dominated officer corps of the times. In contrast to the black rank and file who "worked, went to school, drank, gambled, and frequented the Strip together," black West Point cadets and officers "were in the tradition of the army discouraged from fraternizing with the enlisted men and at the same time not fully accepted by their white fellow officers."

Despite this ambivalent situation, Lieutenant Young was not overwhelmed by the caste system that separated enlisted personnel from those who held a commission. After he received his commission in 1889, Young likewise won over his subordinates. In fact, one of his West Point classmates maintained: "He loved his men and they loved him." As evidence of the esteem Young enjoyed among the rank and file one contemporary wrote:

> ... it was not an uncommon sight to see him at the piano in his army quarters, surrounded by a happy group of his men, entertaining and being entertained. He possessed their sincere respect as well as their affectionate regard.

When Young died in 1922, a white classmate penned highly complementary words in the *Annual Report of the Association of Graduates of the United States Military Academy at West Point* for that year. The obituary ended with words that Young would not have heard during the four years of disconcerting silence he endured at West Point, praising the man who at death was the first black in the United States Army to pin on colonel's eagles:

...he has left as a heritage the fine example of an honorable, efficient, and upright life, remarkable in its spirit of service and of sacrifice for duty, honor, and country. Though life was often pathetically difficult for him in its problems of environment, he lived up to the best traditions of his Alma Mater, and played the game as a worthy graduate of the greatest of military academies. Perhaps the best that can be said of him is that in all his relations with society, both as citizen and soldier, his constructive influence with his people was ever a potent factor along the troublous highway of enlightened progress. (Rhodes 1922, 152)

Charles Young rose to the rank of captain in the Ninth United States Cavalry in the early twentieth century. He would retire as a colonel, but be denied the possibility of a general's star due to a medical retirement prior to World War I.
United States Military History Institute

Benjamin O. Davis Sr. and Early Black Officers

While at Fort Duchesne, Charles Young encountered an ambitious soldier by the name of Benjamin O. Davis. He helped the able soldier prepare for the examination to obtain his commission, a feat that was rare in the military of the era.

Lt. Young's coaching was just one manifestation of the tutoring required to prepare black recruits for military life. Many of the men—both black and white—who came into Uncle Sam's army immediately after the Civil War could not read or write.

Davis ultimately achieved his goal and passed his demanding exam to obtain a lieutenancy. Some forty years later, he would become the first black to earn a general's star, while his son, Benjamin O. Davis Jr., followed in the family tradition and gained fame in his own right as one of the legendary Tuskegee Airmen, which led to his pinning on the three stars of a lieutenant general before retiring from a distinguished career with the United States Air Force.

Black Officers in the Union Army (1862–1865)

Unit	Lt. Cpt.	Maj.	Surgeon	Chaplain	Total	
4th USCI	1		1	2		
54th Mass	3		1	4		
55th Mass	3		2	5		
73rd USCI	17	12	29			
74th USCI	20	10	1	31		
75th USCI	9	7	16			
104th USCI	1		1	2		
Douglas's Battery	2	1	3			
Other Units	7		9	16		
Total	54	31	2	8	13	108

Benjamin O. Davis Sr. was a rare example of an enlisted man commissioned from the ranks. He earned a second lieutenancy in the Tenth United States Cavalry and eventually climbed the military ladder to become the first black United States Army general.

In 1884, Henry V. Plummer received his appointment as the Ninth United States Cavalry's regimental chaplain, thereby becoming the first black clergyman to be commissioned as a chaplain in the regular Army. *Moorland-Springarn Research Center, Howard University*

Chapter 6
CHRISTIAN SOLDIERS
Chaplains

Chaplain Allensworth had this photo taken in his officer's
overcoat in the mid to late 1890s. *Anthony Powell*

In this portrait taken around 1903, Chaplain Allensworth sports shoulder straps displaying the Latin cross that was adopted in 1898, much as he had called for several years earlier. The Latin cross remains the insignia of Christian chaplains in the United States armed forces to the present day. *NARA*

Allen Allensworth's uniform coat from the early twentieth century. *Arizona Historical Society*

O.   45°

Voucher No.   .

Paid _August 31th_, 187 3,

M. J. Gonzales

Chaplain 9th Cav.

From _July 31st_, 187 3,

To _August 31st 1873_

Pay 1873, $ _137 50_

O.   4

Voucher No.   .

Paid _4th Aug._, 187 3,

John N. Schultz

Chaplain 24th Inf.

From _30 June_, 187 3,

To _31 July_ 187 3

Pay 1874, $ _137 50_

The United States,   (No. 3.)

To _M.J. Gonzales Chaplain 9th Cav._ , Dr.

SALARY.	FROM—	TO—	MONTHS.	PAY, PER YEAR.	AMOUNT.
for over _five_ years service.	the _1st_ of _August_, 1873,	the _31st_ of _August_ 1873.	_one_		137 50
					$137, 50

n leave of absence since _____ under S. O., No. ____ , dated Headquarters _____   Deduct half pay for _____ months

_____   Extended by S. O., No. ____ , dated Headquarters _____   _____ days leave of absence.

Returned to duty _____

I certify, on honor, that the amounts charged in the foregoing account are correct and just, as authorized by law, and that they are rightfully due me as stated; and that I am not in arrears with the United States on any account whatsoever. I was last paid to _31st_ _July_, 187 3, by Paymaster _Major Clarke P.M. U.S.A_ and I acknowledge to have received, this _31st_ day of _August_ 1873 of Paymaster _D.W._ _Nicholls_, _____, U. S. A., in full of this account, the sum of _One hundred & thirty_ dollars, __/100 y check No. _cash_ -on _____

(Signed in duplicate.)

M.J. Gonzales
Chaplain 9th Cav. U.S.

When the regiments with black enlisted personnel were originally formed white chaplains such as M.J Gonzales of the Ninth United States Cavalry and John N. Schultz of the Twenty-fourth United States Infantry (whose pay vouchers indicated the sums they received for their services) were sent to minster to them. *George M. Langellier Jr.*

When regimental chaplains were not available sometimes post chaplains served the troops' spiritual needs, as this military man of the cloth depicts in an atypical situation where he has joined a battalion of the Twenty-fifth United States Infantry for dress parade at Fort Shaw, Montana, in the 1890s. *Montana State Historical Society, Helena*

Civil War Chaplains

Henry Plummer was not the first black to serve as a chaplain in the US military. During the Civil War some fourteen men ministered to Union volunteer troops.

Name	Denomination	Unit
Jeremiah Asher	Baptist	6th US Colored Troops
Francis A. Boyd	Christian	109th US Colored Troops
Samuel Harrison	Congregational	54th Massachusetts Infantry (Colored)
William H. Hunter	African Methodist Episcopal 4th US Colored Troops	
William Jackson	Baptist	55th Massachusetts Infantry (Colored)
Chauncey Leonard	Baptist	L'Ouverture Hospital Alexandria, VA
George W. Levere	Congregational	20th US Colored Troops
Benjamin F. Randolph	Presbyterian	26th US Colored Troops
David Stevens	African Methodist Episcopal 36th US Colored Troops	
Henry M. Turner	1st US Colored Troops	
James Underdue	Baptist	39th US Colored Troops
William Waring	Baptist	102nd US Colored Troops
Garland H. White	African Methodist Episcopal 28th US Colored Troops	

During the 1890s, post Chaplain I. Newton Ritner conducted religious services for both black and white members of his Fort Keogh, Montana, parishioners. *Christian Barthelmess Family*

Company K, Twenty-fourth Infantry's quartermaster sergeant stands next to a riddled silhouette target to drive home the point that he was a dead shot with his .30-.40 caliber Krag rifle, c. 1900. A turn of the century ditty that was indicative of the jingoistic mood of the times boasted, "we will civilize them with a Krag," whether in Cuba, the Philippines, or elsewhere, as the United States emerged as an international power. *George M. Langellier Jr.*

Chapter 7

HOT TIME IN THE OLD TOWN

From the Spanish-American War to Desegregation, 1898–1948

Pvt. Fitz Lee of Troop M, Tenth United States Cavalry, hailed from Dinwiddie County, Virginia. His extraordinary performance under fire in Cuba earned him the Medal of Honor, but medical issues led to his early discharge from service in 1900. *Anthony Powell*

The boomtowns Dyea and Skagway, Alaska, required troops to maintain order. In 1899, Company L, Twenty-fourth United States Infantry was on hand to keep the peace in the rough and tumble gold rush region. *National Park Service*

Even a decade after the American frontier was thought to be closed men of the Ninth United States Cavalry were still required to maintain their equestrian skills, as seen here in 1900. *Anthony Powell*

The band of the Ninth United States Cavalry ready for practice at Fort D. A. Russell, Wyoming, in 1911. *Wyoming State Museum*

From 1908 to 1913, Fort Ethan Allen, Vermont, housed the Tenth United States Cavalry, including men from the machine gun platoon. This weapon ultimately contributed to the obsolescence of mounted combat troops. *George M. Langellier Jr.*

171

Farrier Silas Johnson was with Troop D, Tenth United States Cavalry in Cuba. President William McKinley shook the young veteran's hand to congratulate him when he returned stateside. Johnson remained with the regiment and was sent to Fort Robinson, Nebraska, where he and his wife would announce the arrival of a son who was born on February 10, 1906. *University of Vermont*

Mitchell A. Harris was a band member at Fort Robinson, Nebraska, when the Tenth Cavalry served there between 1892–1900 before being transferred to the Philippines. *Moorland-Spingarn Research Center, Howard University*

were among the first killed in the charge. Stopped by the fierce fire from the Mexicans, the black horse soldiers quickly dismounted and returned fire. The cavalrymen became confused. Ammunition was nearly exhausted. Realizing that defeat was imminent, the greatly outnumbered survivors beat a hasty retreat. Nevertheless, they managed to inflict over eighty casualties on the Mexicans while suffering less than one-fourth that number killed and wounded from their own ranks. While giving a good account of themselves, the survivors nonetheless became prisoners of war.

In addition to the defeat, Boyd's recklessness at Carrizal nearly sparked a war between the United States and Mexico. Citizens on both sides of the border clamored for revenge, but government leaders ignored the warmongering. Mexican officials had their hands full with Villa in the north and Emiliano Zapata in the south, while Wilson realized that the United States would probably enter the raging European conflict soon. Both sides began negotiating the details for Pershing's evacuation from Mexico. Finally, after eleven months of wandering through northern Mexico, Wilson recalled the dejected American troops to the United States. The country's military might was needed far across the Atlantic with the United States' entry into World War I.

While blacks were sent to Europe, most of the units dispatched to France served as support troops, rather than in combat. Those who fought in the trenches were not from the regular Army. In fact, the black regulars remained stateside, such as the Twenty-fourth United States Infantry with elements scattered at posts such as a battalion at Camp Logan in Houston, Texas. Some of the residents' fear of armed blacks erupted in August 1917. The appearance of black servicemen stirred racist feelings among white Houstonians, who hurled insults at them and began strictly enforcing the town's Jim Crow laws. Angered by this abuse some of the black foot soldiers purposely disobeyed segregation ordinances. In response, local police harassed and arrested these protesters for their insolence, increasing already hostile tensions. Racial strains finally snapped on August 23, when a rumor (later revealed to be false) spread throughout the black camp that policemen had shot two of their comrades. More than 100 soldiers responded, forcibly seizing rifles and ammunition from the armory and angrily marching into Houston to seek vengeance. In the ensuing shoot-out two black soldiers and seventeen white civilians were killed. Many more were wounded.

The army's response was to place sixty-four black soldiers on trial at Fort Sam Houston, San Antonio, for murder and mutiny. Subsequent investigations implicated additional members of the battalion. Military authorities quietly executed sixteen soldiers and sentenced another sixty-five to life in prison. Even though enforcement of segregation laws played a leading role in inciting this outbreak, Secretary of War Newton Baker attempted to appease white Southerners by advising all commanders of black troops to order their men to obey racially restricting Jim Crow laws.

1st Lt. O.J.W. Scott became the regimental chaplain of the Twenty-fifth United States Infantry. He would eventually transfer to the Tenth United States Cavalry. *Anthony Powell*

Following the armistice that brought the "war to end all wars" to a conclusion, no repetition of the magnitude of the Houston clash occurred. Nevertheless, black soldiers continued to face racial discrimination. Stationed largely at Georgia's Fort Benning, Arizona's Fort Huachuca, and Kansas' Forts Riley and Leavenworth, the four black regiments (Twenty-fourth and Twenty-fifth Infantry and the Ninth and Tenth Cavalry) were reduced to grooming horses and performing other fatigue duties, with the exception of those troops stationed along the troubled border between Mexico and the United States. In fact, as late as 1930, troopers of the Tenth Cavalry clashed with Mexican forces, indicating that despite Villa's demise at the hands of assassins the two countries were uneasy neighbors.

This exchange would be the regiment's final combat laurels as a mounted unit. In 1931, after more than six decades in the saddle, the Tenth Cavalry would have its horses taken away and the once proud cavalrymen would be scattered to many installations to perform tasks that were more menial than military. At that point, the Tenth was a regiment in name only. Leaving Fort Huachuca for the last time was a sad day in the unit's history, as Vance Marchbanks, one of the Tenth Cavalry's few black officers, recorded in his unpublished recollections (now preserved at the Fort Huachuca Museum):

> One day the inevitable happened, the War Department decided that the horse cavalry was outmoded. One of the first regiments to be disbanded was the colored tenth. We loaded our horses on the freight cars and sent them away. Next day the Pullman sleepers backed quietly into the rail yard. The colored troops boarded the train with tears in their eyes and started their trip north to become service detachments at various post schools.

As another indication of the deteriorating post-World War I climate, few opportunities to be commissioned in the regular army existed for black aspirants. For example, only one black, Benjamin O. Davis Jr., graduated from West Point between 1920 and 1940. During this same period, only five black commissioned officers were in the regular Army: two line officers and three chaplains (Louis

Keeping fit and ready for combat meant plenty of practice, including with bayonets for peacetime members of the Twenty-fifth United States Infantry, Company M, at Fort Huachuca, Arizona, in 1928. *Fort Huachuca Museum*

During December 1943, 180 women from the Thirty-second and Thirty-third Women's Army Auxiliary Corps (WAAC) detrained and arrived at Fort Huachuca, Arizona, thereby ushering in a new chapter in the history of blacks in the United States Army in the West. *Fort Huachuca Museum*

Carter, Tenth Cavalry; W. W. Gladden, Twenty-fourth Infantry; and O. J. W. Scott, Twenty-fifth Infantry).

Even the existence of the black regiments came in to question. Beginning in 1919, the army prohibited enlisting blacks other than those who had served in the military prior to April. In 1921, six troops of the Ninth Cavalry and seven of the Tenth Cavalry were demobilized, leaving the two regiments with a skeleton force.

The remaining personnel were often converted from veteran fighting men to service units, relegated to truck drivers, janitors, maintenance workers, warehousemen, cooks, clerks, carpenters, messengers, and other chores, such as serving as officers' servants, including duties as equitation instructors for the families of their white commanders—becoming little more than domestics.

With the 1926 creation of the Air Corps (from which blacks were barred), a cap on overall army strength meant more drawdowns were on the horizon that would possibly lead to the disbandment of two or more black regiments, sacrificing them to provide openings for the Air Corps. While that rumored action never came to pass, the Tenth Cavalry and Twenty-fifth Infantry in particular were sent piecemeal to posts, much as the regiments and battalions were dispersed after World War I. Ultimately, in 1944, the Tenth Cavalry did disappear from the war department's rolls. Even before the regiment's elimination, the number of blacks in the regular Army had dwindled to 3,640 men, a small fraction of the military force in 1939. Such was the status of blacks in the Army as war clouds rained

Gen. Colin Powell acknowledged he and others stood on the shoulders of the buffalo soldiers when he gave the keynote address at the dedication of the monument at Fort Leavenworth, Kansas.

down on December 7, 1941, at Pearl Harbor.

That picture changed dramatically with the entry of the United States in World War II. By 1942, there were 467,883 blacks in the Army, which two years later soared to 701,678; four years after Pearl Harbor blacks totaled 8.81% of the Army's overall strength, including two divisions manned by blacks (the 92nd and 93rd), both of which had been raised, trained, and deployed from Fort Huachuca, which in many respects came to be the final home for African American men and women in the Army uniform during the era of segregation.

The long-standing "separate but equal" formula began to disappear. With President Harry S. Truman's 1948 issuance of Executive Order 9981, integration of the US armed forces began to change the face of the nation's military. The World War II "Double V" goal of the black community in the United States to achieve victory over fascism abroad and racism

A detail from the Twenty-fourth United States Infantry have been supplied mounts in 1899 to assist them in patrolling Yosemite National Park. *Yosemite Research Library National Park Service*

at home began to become a reality. Over the ensuing decades discrimination dwindled, albeit not disappearing. As the civil rights movement gained momentum and fulfilled the quest for equality and freedom bought with the blood of generations of black soldiers, a new day was coming that paved the way for Colin Powell's assumption as the chairman of the joint chiefs of staff and in some respects the election of Barack Obama as commander in chief.

The National Parks

After returning from Cuba in 1898, black troops served at far flung assignments from Vermont to Alaska, and even in Hawaii and the Philippines. As was the case with their white comrades, they were occasionally dispatched to Yosemite and Sequoia national parks, where between 1891 and 1913, US Army personnel carried on the role later played by National Park Service rangers. During the summer months, detachments usually consisting of two troops or companies of approximately sixty men each under their commanding officers—who became acting military superintendents—were assigned to each park. These units would be men drawn from either the Twenty-fourth Infantry or Ninth Cavalry.

Among them was Charles Young, the third black graduate of the United States Military Academy. In 1903, Cpt. Young served as the acting military superintendent of Sequoia National Park; because of this detail he is considered by some to be the first black superintendent of a national park. With Troops I and M of the Ninth United States Cavalry—a number of whom fought in the Philippines—Young's men were kept busy "confiscating firearms as well as curbing poaching of the park's wildlife, suppressing wildfires, ending illegal grazing of livestock on federal lands, and stopping thefts of timber and other natural objects. They oversaw the construction of roads, trails, and other infrastructure." (www.nps.gov/chyo/learn)

In 1903, Charles Young commanded men detailed from the Ninth United States Cavalry dispatched to Yosemite National Park. *Yosemite Research Library National Park Service*

Ninth United States Cavalry troopers from the Presidio of San Francisco stand atop the Fallen Monarch in Yosemite's Mariposa Grove in 1904. *Yosemite Research Library National Park Service*

Many theories exist about the origin of the term "buffalo soldier," among them the contention the name stemmed from the buffalo overcoats issued to troops in cold climates. Like many of the other explanations, this reasoning has no basis in fact. Indeed, such foul weather gear was not provided to black troops until they served on the northern plains many years after the expression had appeared in a number of printed sources. *Herb Peck Jr.*

Chapter 8

BUFFALO SOLDIERS—WHEN WILL THEY CALL YOU A MAN?

History and Heritage

Budding eastern artist Fredrick Remington received a boost to his career with the publication of his rendering of the dramatic rescue of Cpl. Edward Scott of the Tenth United States Cavalry that appeared on the cover of the popular periodical *Harper's Weekly* August 21, 1886. As an indication of the bias of the era, the young lieutenant who helped saved Scott's life, Powhattan Clarke, received the Medal of Honor for this exploit and considerable press, while the black trooper who assisted him never had his name recorded, much less was presented with a Medal of Honor for his valor under fire.

THE BUFFALO SOLDIER
FORT HUACHUCA HONORS THE BUFFALO
SOLDIER, A SYMBOL OF THE PROUD
TRADITION OF THE BLACK FIGHTING MAN
AND REMEMBERS THE PROMINENT ROLE HE
HAS PLAYED IN THE POST'S HISTORY.
3 MARCH 1977
ARTIST: ROSE MURRAY

Many monuments (such as Rose Murray's bronze at Fort Huachuca), museums, historic sites, veterans' groups, and reenactors have sprung up to foster both the reality and myth of the buffalo soldier. *Fort Huachuca Museum*

Even while the Tenth United States Cavalry was an active horse-mounted unit prior to World War II, the regiment drew on its history. Here the regimental color guard forms (c. 1940) and are essentially attired as the first troopers would have been in 1866. This group was the forerunner to reenactors that would follow decades later.

the vernacular. Eventually popular culture also embraced the image of the buffalo soldier. Fiction, film, and television added to the growing reputation of the blacks who wore Army blue in the old West.

Furthermore, reenactors, historic sites, museums, and monuments from Kansas to California pay tribute to the history and sometimes the legend of the black frontier soldier. Likewise, there are occasional musical tributes, such as the 1974 *Soul Saga* (*Song of the Buffalo Soldier*) produced by Quincy Jones and the 1983 reggae cult classic *Buffalo Soldier* by Bob Marley and King Sporty.

In addition, scores of modern day artists have followed in the footsteps of Fredric Remington's renderings from the late 1880s. Indeed, 150 years after the US Congress created the black regiments their once obscure existence has been woven into the national fabric as a significant part of American history. As a video tribute produced by Texas Parks and Wildlife concluded, "It seems ironic…their greatest victory may be in the present fought not with bullets, but with a legacy of honor, courage, and integrity." Frank N. Schubert phrased the significance of the black frontier soldier another way, "It's not just black history; it's American history." As he went on to conclude, "The buffalo soldier story, which blends history and heritage; fact with myth, has entered the mainstream with other iconic western sagas…."

Hollywood Buffalo Soldiers

While during the late nineteenth century mentions of black soldiers occasionally appeared in print or were periodically subjects for Fredric Remington, their exploits were not common knowledge. Even the presence of a few black horsemen (presumably veterans) in William F. "Buffalo Bill" Cody's Congress of Rough Riders did little to spread the fame of the so-called buffalo soldiers.

Cody's rip roaring live traveling show helped pave the way for the motion picture, another entertainment form that gave rise to the western and a staple of the American film industry that spawned Hollywood. Yet "Tinsel Town" was not the only place where movies were made. One unlikely silent era film center, Omaha, Nebraska, served as the headquarters of the Lincoln Film Company. A pair of black siblings, George and Noble Johnson, headed this production studio. The Johnson brothers released features about blacks for a segregated black audience.

One of their earliest efforts, *A Trooper of Troop K*, appeared in 1917. It was billed as "A Thrilling Picturization of the Late Carrizal, Mexico Battle, Between the Fighting U.S. Tenth Cavalry and Carranzist's Soldiers" during the Mexican Revolution. The plot revolved around an irresponsible young man whose inability to hold a job earns him the nickname "Shiftless Joe" (Noble Johnson). A society girl named Clara Holmes (Beulah Hall) sees something in Joe and encourages him to enlist. Joe joins the Tenth Cavalry, becomes a model trooper, and even

While Remington was sharing his artistic vision of the frontier, William F. "Buffalo Bill" Cody also created his version of the Wild West, replete with his "Congress of Rough Riders." Occasionally Cody trotted out black cavalrymen in his troupe decked out in reasonably accurate regulation dress regalia of the late 1800s. It is not certain whether the four men thus attired were veterans portraying African American horse soldiers or just members from Cody's road company. *Anthony Powell*

rescues his white commanding officer during an intense battle with 300 extras as Mexican forces. Joe has become a hero and can return to marry the leading lady.

Given that the Tenth Cavalry had formed part of Pershing's Punitive Expedition into Mexico, *A Trooper of Troop K* resonated with viewers familiar with the headlines of the day. In 1922, the Johnsons sought to return to the Tenth Cavalry as a theme, but in this instance did not take inspiration from current affairs. Instead, the Johnsons crafted a script about a disillusioned World War I veteran who returns from France and regains his sense of self worth by helping the regiment combat drug traffickers smuggling opium across the border from Mexico.

While the scenario was contrived, remarkably the storyline is one that could resonate with twenty-first century filmgoers. The picture's appeal was a moot point, however, because Lincoln Films folded in 1922. The proposed picture never reached the silver screen, although the company did shoot two reels of the Tenth Cavalry at Fort Huachuca, perhaps as "B-roll" for the feature.

More than two decades passed before another black production company returned to the subject of African American soldiers in the West. With World War II in full swing Spencer Williams (perhaps best known for his role as Andrew H. Brown in CBS's early 1950s *Amos and Andy* television series and supposedly

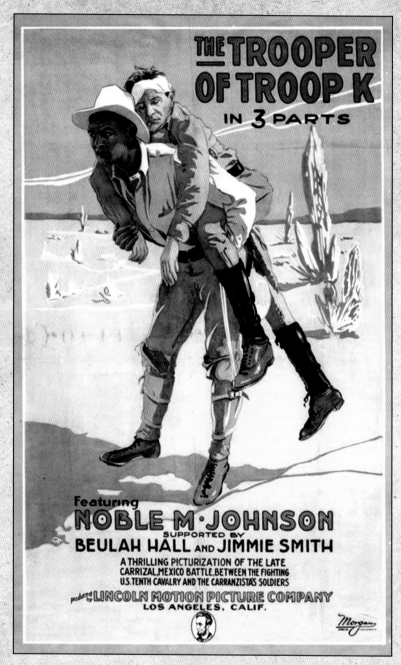

The Johnson brothers formed a film production company to make movies for segregated black audiences. Their silent features carried messages to uplift the "race" as in *Trooper of Troop K* about a troubled, no account young man whose stint with the cavalry on the border changed his life, turning him into a hero. *University of California Los Angeles Library Digital Collections*

Released in 1959, *The Wonderful Country* depicted black troops serving in Texas in a matter of fact manner, rather than dwelling on their presence as a significant plot element. Baseball immortal Leroy "Satchel" Paige was cast as a calm, competent cavalry sergeant playing opposite the film's star, Robert Mitchum. *United Artists*

a veteran of the border war with Pershing) directed *Marching On* (also known as *Where's My Man Tonight*) in 1943 for Bourgeois-Jenkins. Shirker Rodney Tucker Jr. (Hugo Martin) is the son and grandson of black veterans, but he wants to avoid military service. He deserts, but redeems himself by thwarting Japanese fifth columnists. In the process he is reunited with his long lost father (played by John Hemmings) and wins the girl. In some respects this low budget melodrama was reminiscent of the lost nitrate *A Trooper of Troop K*. Although the later film may not be memorable, it did offer one important element, in that many of the scenes were filmed at Fort Huachuca during the war.

Eventually frontier black soldiers figured into the post Second World War mainstream cinema and television lineup. At first, 1959's *Wonderful Country* (United Artists) was a matter of fact representation of black troops set in the turbulent times of 1860s' Mexico. A brief segment of the show included US forces along the border. Rather than make a self-conscious statement, the cavalrymen are African Americans under a thoroughly professional non-commissioned officer, Sgt. Tobe Sutton, portrayed by baseball legend Leroy "Satchel" Paige. Interestingly, there is no in-depth explanation of the presence of black troopers rather than the typical white cavalrymen seen in scores of other Hollywood oaters.

In that same year a more focused effort appeared as an episode of *Dick Powell's Zane Grey Theater* CBS western anthology series. This pioneer production titled

195

Although not usually remembered for his dramatic portrayals, Sammy Davis Jr. turned in a reputable performance as a racist black non-commissioned officer faced with a life and death struggle in a 1959 episode of *Dick Powell's Zane Grey Theater*. *CBS*

"Incident of the Buffalo Soldier" brought Woody Strode back to the topic of black cavalrymen in the West in a 1961 *Rawhide* show with a young Clint Eastwood. *CBS*

Sgt.s Three (1962) was a far cry from *Sgt. Rutledge*. Once again Sammy Davis Jr. was in front of the camera, but now as a tongue and cheek character patterned on Rudyard Kipling's faithful regimental beasty Gunga Din. *United Artists*

FRANK SINATRA DEAN MARTIN
PETER LAWFORD SAMMY DAVIS JR. JOEY BISHOP SERGEANTS 3

Yaphet Kotto made a guest appearance alongside series regular Leif Erickson in a 1968 "The Buffalo Soldiers" episode of *The High Chaparral. NBC*

In 1964, William Marshall appeared as a black non-commissioned officer on yet another *Rawhide* show, in this instance titled "Incident at Seven Fingers." *CBS*

"The Buffalo Soldiers" portrayed a detachment of black horse soldiers under Sgt. Morgan (James Edwards) sent to escort a Comanche leader to sign a peace treaty. The detail's second in command, Cpl. Smith (Sammy Davis Jr.), loathes Indians, but after an attack by Apaches in which Morgan is killed, the corporal takes charge and refuses to surrender the Comanche to his enemies.

Years later, Davis was again cast in a part inspired by black soldiers in the west, this time as a civilian want-to-be bugler in the Rat Pack's tongue in cheek take on *Gunga Din*.

The 1962 *Sergeants 3* was a typical slapstick romp for the cast, but this was not so as far as an earlier big screen release directed by John Ford in 1960. *Sergeant Rutledge* was a serious and ground breaking (for its time) portrayal of the black frontier soldier. Woody Strode as stalwart Ninth United States Cavalry 1st Sgt. Braxton Rutledge flees after being falsely charged of rape and a double murder. His commanding officer defends him after the sergeant's capture and return for court martial. The dialogue includes the lore that the Plains Indians called the blacks "buffalo soldiers" because when they first saw black troops they were wearing buffalo coats and caps in winter.

By 1961, to a certain degree Strode would reprise his earlier appearance as a stoic black non-commissioned officer Cpl. Gabe Washington in an episode of the television series *Rawhide* ("Incident of the Buffalo Soldier"). Unlike his character in the 1960 film, Strode is not exonerated for killing in self-defense. Instead, he is hunted down and shot to death by the patrol sent to bring him back to the fort.

Strode was also slated to return as a model top sergeant in a proposed sequel to *Sergeant Rutledge*. Under the working title "The Black Lieutenant," Strode as a seasoned NCO was to be pitted against the first black West Point graduate for the affections of the leading lady. The subtheme of this unproduced feature revolved around a Gatling gun that would be the main emphasis for a later movie *The Gatling Gun* (1971), in which Strode appeared as a supporting actor.

Although "The Black Lieutenant" was never filmed, a 1964 episode of *Rawhide* ("Incident at Seven Fingers") resurrected a subject that was becoming cliché. A tough black sergeant (William Marshall) is falsely accused of cowardice and

Woody Strode in the 1960 courtroom centered *Sgt. Rutledge.* On the witness stand the title character explodes "I am a man!" as his defense council and badgering prosecutor flank him. *Warner Bros*

Screened under many titles from *Soul Soldier* to *Red, White, and Black* and in re-release as *Buffalo Soldiers*, the ensemble of this 1970 oater gathered at Fort Davis National Historic Site for on location shooting. *Hirschman/Northern Productions*

Above: The cast of *Buffalo Soldiers*—a 1979 pilot for an unsuccessful TV series—included Richard Lawson (Caleb); Charles Robinson (Pvt. Wright); Ralph Wilcox (Oakley); Hilly Hicks (Willie); John Beck (Col. Frank "Buckshot" O'Connor); and Stan Shaw (Sgt. Joshua Haywood). *MGM Television/NBC*

Left: In 1997, Danny Glover followed in Woody Strode's footsteps as a black first sergeant pitted against prejudice and Apaches, but the Indians are not necessarily the enemy in the made for television *Buffalo Soldiers*. *TNT*

One of Danny Glover's costumes from *Buffalo Soldiers*.
Sharlot Hall Museum

of Graduate of the United States Military Academy Annual Report, June 12. 1922. Saginaw, MI: Seeman & Peters, Inc. Printers and Binders, 1922. 152.

Robinson, Charles M. III. *The Court Martial of Lieutenant Henry Flipper.* El Paso: The University of Texas at El Paso, 1994.

_____. *The Fall of a Black Officer: Racism and the Myth of Henry O. Flipper.* Norman: University of Oklahoma Press, 2008.

Shellum, Brian G. *Black Cadet in a White Bastion: Charles Young at West Point.* Lincoln: University of Nebraska Press, 2006.

_____. *Black Officer in a Buffalo Soldier Regiment: The Military Career of Charles Young.* Lincoln: University of Nebraska Press, 2010.

CHAPTER 6: CHRISTIAN SOLDIERS

Powell, Anthony. *Black Chaplains In The US Army 1862–1945.* San Jose, CA: Portraits In Black Ltd., 1994.

Langellier, John P. and Osur, Alan M. *Chaplain Allen Allensworth and the 24th Infantry 1886–1906.* Tucson: Tucson Corral of the Westerners, Inc., 1980.

Seraile, William. *Voice of Dissent: Theophilus Gould Steward (1843–1924) and Black America.* Brooklyn, NY: Carlson Publishing Inc., 1991.

Stover, Earl F. *Up From Handymen: The United States Army Chaplaincy 1865–1920.* Washington, DC: Office of the Chief of Chaplains, 1977.

_____. *Chaplain Henry V. Plummer, His Ministry and His Court Martial.* Lincoln: Nebraska Historical Society, 1975.

CHAPTER 7: HOT TIME IN THE OLD TOWN

Cashin, Herschel V. *Under Fire with the Tenth U.S. Cavalry.* Niwot: University Press of Colorado, 1993.

Christian, Garna L. *Black Soldiers in Jim Crow Texas 1899–1917.* College Station: Texas A&M University Press, 1995.

Cooper, Michael L. *Double V Campaign: African Americans and World War II.* New York: Lodestar Books, 1998.

Egloff, Franklin R. *Theodore Roosevelt, An American Portrait.* New York: Vantage Press, 1980. 126.

Ellis, Mark. *Race War and Surveillance: African Americans and the United States*

Government during World War I. Bloomington and Indianapolis: Indiana University Press, 2001.

Fletcher, Marvin A. *The Black Soldier and Officer in the United States Army 1891–1917*. Columbia: University of Missouri Press, 1974.

Gatewood, Willard B. Jr. *Smoked Yankees and the Struggle for Empire: Letters from Negro Soldiers 1898–1902*. Urbana: University of Illinois Press, 1971.

James, Jennifer C. *A Freedom Bought with Blood: African American War Literature from the Civil War to World War II*. Chapel Hill: University of North Carolina Press, 2007.

James, Rawn, Jr. *The Double V: How Wars, Protest, and Harry Truman Desegregated America's Military*. New York: Bloomsbury Press, 2013.

Johnson, Edward Austin. *History of the Negro Regiments in the Spanish American War: And Other Items of Interest*. Raleigh: Capital Printing Co., 1899. 61.

Knapp, George E. *Buffalo Soldiers at Fort Leavenworth in the 1930s and Early 1940s*. Ft. Leavenworth: U.S. Army Command and General Staff College, 1991.

Lee, Ulysses. *The Employment of Negro Troops*. Washington, DC: Office of the Chief of Military History, 1966.

Lynk, Miles Vandahurst. *The Black Troopers: Or, the Daring Heroism of the Negro Soldiers in the Spanish-American War*. New York: AMS Press, 1971.

MacGregor, Morris J. *Integration of the Armed Forces, 1940–1965*. Washington, DC: Center of Military History, 1981.

MacGregor, Morris J. and Bernard Nalty, eds. *Blacks in the United States Armed Forces: Basic Documents 13 vols*. Washington, DC: Scholarly Resources, 1977. 3, 224–25.

Meyerson, Harvey. *Nature's Army: When Soldiers Fought for Yosemite*. Lawrence: University Press of Kansas, 2001.

Morehouse, Maggi M. *Fighting in the Jim Crow Army: Black Men and Women Remember World War II*. Lanham, MD: Rowman & Littlefield Publishers, Inc., 2000.

Powell, Anthony. *For the Love of Liberty the African American Soldier in the US Army 1898–1902*. Vol. 2. San Jose, CA: Portraits In Black Ltd., 1996.

_____. *For the Love of Liberty the African American Soldier in the US Army 1903–1916*. Vol. 3. San Jose, CA: Portraits In Black Ltd., 1996.

_____. *For the Love of Liberty the African American Soldier in the US Army 1917–1940*. Vol. 4. San Jose, CA: Portraits In Black Ltd., 1996.

Rawn, James Jr. *The Double V: How Wars, Protest, and Harry Truman Desegregated America's Military*. New York: Bloomsbury Press, 2013.

Scott, Edward Van Zile. *Unwept Unhonored Unsung: Black American Soldiers & the Spanish-American War*. Montgomery: Black Belt Press, 1995.

Scott, Emmett J. *Scott's Official History of the American Negro in the World War.* Chicago: Homewood Press, 1919.

Slotkin, Richard. *Lost Battalions: The Great War and the Crisis of American Nationalists*. New York: Henry Holt and Company, 2005.

Smith, Stephen D. *The African American Soldier at Fort Huachuca, Arizona 1892–1946*. Seattle: U.S. Army Corps of Engineers, 2001.

Weaver, John D. *The Brownsville Raid*. College Station: Texas A&M University Press, 1992.

CHAPTER 8: BUFFALO SOLDIERS

Bellah, James Warner. *Sergeant Rutledge*. New York: Bantam Books, 1960.

Berry, S. Torriano with Berry, Venise T. *The 50 Most Influential Black Films: A Celebration of African-American Talent, Determination, and Creativity*. New York: Kensington Publishing Corp., 2001.

Bohjalian, Chris. *The Buffalo Soldier*. New York: Vintage Contemporaries, 2002.

Copeland, Martin. *Right Proud: The Buffalo Soldiers*. Booklocker.com Incorporated, 2002.

Downey, Fairfax. *Indian-Fighting Army*. New York: Charles Scribner's Sons, 1941.

Goodman, Charles B. *The Buffalo Soldier*. Los Angeles: Holloway House Publishing Company, 1993.

Hayes, Rebecca O. *Private Cathy's Secret*. NP: Rebecca O. Hayes, 2010.

Heuman, William. *Buffalo Soldier*. New York: Dodd, Mead & Company, 1969.

Kelton, Elmer. *The Wolf and the Buffalo*. New York: Bantam Books, 1980.

Place, J.A. *The Western Films of John Ford*. Secaucus, NJ: The Citadel Press, 1974.

Prebble, John. *The Buffalo Soldiers*. London: Transworld Publishers, 1959.

Robert, J.B. *The Gunsmith Buffalo Soldiers* (#362) New York: Penguin, 2012.

Roe, Frances. M. *Army Letters from and Officer's Wife*. Lincoln: University of Nebraska Press, 1981.

Samuels, Peggy and Harold. Eds. *The Collected Writings of Fredric Remington*. Garden City, NY: Doubleday, 1979.

Smith, Cornelius C., Jr. *Fort Huachuca: The Story of a Frontier Post*. Washington, DC: Government Printing Office, 1976.

Splete, Allen P. and Marilyn D. Eds. *Fredric Remington—Selected Letters*. New York: Abbeville Press, 1988.

Stroode, Woody and Young, Sam. *Goal Dust: The Warm and Candid Memoirs of a Pioneer Black Athlete and Actor*. Lanham, MD: Madison Books, 1990.

Yellow Robe, William S. *Grandchildren of the Buffalo Soldiers and Other Untold Stories*. Los Angeles: UCLA American Indian Studies Center, 2009.

Yoggy, Gary A. *Riding the Video Range: The Rise and Fall of the Western on Television*. Jefferson, NC: McFarland & Company Inc., 1995.

Willard, Tom. *Buffalo Soldiers*. New York: A Tom Doherty Associates Book, 1996.

INDEX

African Methodist Episcopa1, 163

Ahumada, Mexico, 175

Alabama, 105; 108;

Alaska, 169-170; 181

Alcohol-Liquor, 153

Alexander, John H., 143-44; 146

Allen, David, 95

Allen, Leona Howard, *95*

Allensworth, Allen, *132*; *153-54*; 155; *156*; 157-58;

Anderson, Aaron, 32

Anderson, Marian, 186

Anderson, Robert, 114

Anderson, William T. ,155; *160*; 161

Andrews, George, *90*

Andrews, George L., 160-61;

Apache, 44; 46-47; 49; 59; 61; *62*; 64-65; 120-21; 135; 141; 198; 200

Apache Kid, 47; 64

Appomattox (Courthouse), VA, 36

Arapaho, 57; 59

Arkansas, 15; 50; 108; 143

Arizona, 47; 49; 61-65; 73; 77; 79; 82; 86; 89-90; 92; 105; 112-13; 128; 131; 177-79; 187-88

Armes, George, 57

Armistead (Sergeant), *62*

Army and Navy Journal, 43; 134; 153; 187

Artillery, *13*; 14; *19*; 50; 78; 108; 133

Asher, Jeremiah, 163

Athletics-Sports, 64; 81; *85*

Attucks, Crispus, 14

Augur, Christopher C., 141

Badie, David, *104*

Baldwin, Frank, 73

Baldwin. T.A., 40

Bands/Music/Trumpeter, 14; 47; *79*; 88; *90*; 93; *95*; *98*; 99; *100-101*; *105*; 107; *171*; *173*; 192;

Bannister (Sergeant), *95*

Baptist, 119; 152; 163

Barber, Merritt, 143

Barnes, William, 32

Beck, John, *200*

Belknap, William, 46

Beaty, Powhatan, *29*; 32

Beecher's Island, CO, 130; 187

Benjamin, Robert, 153

Bentley, George, 126

Benteen, Fredrick W., 43

Bentzoni, Charles, *71*

Bicycle, 73-74; *75*

Biddle, James, 109

Big Flats, NY, 109

Big Foot, 53-54

Bigelow, John, 40; 93; 117

Bivins, Horace Wayman, 126

Blake, Robert, 32

"Bloody Kansas", 13

Blunt, James G., 15

Bonney, William (aka Billy the Kid), 47

"Boomers", 50; *51*

Boston Massacre, 14

Bourgeois-Jenkins Film Productions, 195

Boyd, Charles, 175-76

Boyd, Francis A., 163

Boyne, Thomas, 33; 108

Brice, William H., *103*
Bronson, James H., 32
Brooke, John R., 53
Brown, Annie L., 112
Brown, Benjamin, 73; *105*
Brown, John, 13
Brown, John L., 132
Brown, Marion, 42
Brown, William H., 32
Brown, Wilson, 32
Brownsville, TX, 44; 46; 108; 169; 174
Bruin, Madison, 119
Buell, Mrs. James W., 88
Buffalo Bill Cody Wild West and Congress of Rough Riders, 192-93
Buffalo Soldier, 124; 180; 184-90; 192; 196-202
Bullis, John L., 127
Bunche, Ralph, 186
Burley, Robert, *104*
Burlington Railroad, 55
Butler, Benjamin F., 31
California, 36; 192
Camp
  Bettens, WY, 55-56
  Distribution, VA, 69
  Logan, TX, 176
  Supply, OK, 60
  Wichita, OK, 60
  William Penn, PA, *23*
Carey, Joseph, 55
Carlisle Barracks, PA, 114
Carney, William H., *29*; 32
Carpenter, Louis, 40; 130
Carr, Eugene A., 40
Carrizo Canyon, NM, 121
Carrizal, Mexico, 48-49; 175-76; 192
Carter, Louis, 177; 179

Carter's Ridge, VA, 113
Castle Pinckney, SC, 69
Cathey, William (aka Cathy Williams), 119; 124
Cavalry Regiments
First Volunteer, 169; 202
Third U.S., 48; 132-33
Fourth U.S., 40; 64; 133
Fifth U.S., 48; 132-33
Sixth U.S., 44; 49; 55; 133
Seventh U.S., 53-54; 132-33
Eighth U.S., 55; 132-33
Ninth U.S., 36; *41*; 43-50; *52*; 53-55; *56*; 57; 61; 67; *85*; 88; 93; *95*; *104*;108; *109*; *112*; *116*; *121*; 126; *129*; *131*; 132-33; *134*; 143-44; *147*; *150*; 152-53; *160*; 161; *162*; 169; *170-71*; 177; 179; 181; *182-83*; 186; 198
Tenth U.S., *34*; 36; *37*; 40; *41*; 42-43; 48-49; 57; *58*; 59-61; *63*; 64; *65-66*; 67; 70; 73; 77; 78; *79*; *82-83*; *89*; 93; 99; *100*; 105; *106*; 198, 114; *115*; *117*; *120*; 126-27; *128*; *130*; 132-33; *136*; *139*; 140; 143; *149*; 161; *167*; 169; *171-73*; 175; 177; 179; *185*; 186-187; *188*; 189; *191*; 192-93; 202
Eighteenth Kansas Volunteer, 59
Chaffin's Farm, VA, 29-30
Chaplain's Movement, 153
Charles County, MD, 112
Cherokee Bill (aka Crawford Goldsby), 132
Cheyenne, 57; 59-60; 67; 187; 189; 202;
Cheyenne, WY, 55
Chickamauga, GA, 161
Clarke, Powhattan, *185*
Cleveland, Grover, 154

Spanish American War, 114; 117; 126; 129; 140; 145; 167; 169; 202

Springfield Rifle, 73

Stance, Emanuel, 33; 46

Stevens, David, 163

Starr, Stephen, 108

Steward, Theophilus G., 155; *159*; 160-61;

Stillwater, OK, 50

Strawn, Tom, *19*

"Striker" (aka "Dog Robber"), 81; 90

Strode, Woody, *196*; 198; *199*; 200; 202

Suggs, WY, 55

Sully, Alfred, 73

Sykes, Zekiel, *104*

Taylor, Stephen, *104*

Taylor, Thomas V., 122; *123*; 126

Tennessee, 108; 117

Texas, 44-47; 4; 54; 57; 60-61; 88; 108; 114-15; 118; 126-27; 135; 137; 140-42; 169; 174-75; 192; 195

Texas Ranger, 174

Thomas, George H., 22

Thomas, Lorenzo, 15

Tinaja de las Palmas, 141

Trooper of Troop K, 192-93; *194*; 195

Truman, Harry S, 180

Tularosa Reservation, NM, 49

Turner, Henry M., 163

Turner. Ted, 202

Underdue, James, 163

United States Army Air Corps, 179

United States Colored Troops (USCT) See Cavalry Regiments and Infantry Regiments

United States Military Academy (West Point), NY, 40; 74; 133; 138-40; 143-46; 177; 181; 198

United States Navy, 32; 152-54

USS *Maine*, 168

Utah, 50; 56; 81; 93; 101-02; 143; 146

Ute, 48

Van Peebles, Mario, 202

Veal, Charles, 32

Vermont, 108; 169; 171; 181

Victorio, 47-49; 61; 108-09; 141

Villa, Francisco "Pancho", 174-77

Virginia, 14; 29; 31; 69; 108; 113-14; 118; 126; 167

Walley, Augustus, 33

Waller, Ruben, *130*; 187

Walterboro, SC, 69

Ward, John, 33

Waring, William, 163

Washington, George, 14

Washington, DC, 46; 48; 67; 69; 108; 120; 152

West Virginia, 108

Wham, Joseph, 73; 113

White, Garland H., 163

Whittaker, Johnson Chesnutt, *138*

Wilberforce University, 144

Wilcox, Ralph, *200*

Wild Cat, 135

Wilks, Jacob, 108

Williams, George Washington 114; 126

Williams, Moses, 33

Williams, Spencer, 193

Wilson, George, *104*

Wilson, William O., 33; 54

Wilson, Woodrow, 154; 175-76

Women's Army Auxiliary Corps
  (WAAC), *179*

Wonderful Country, 195

Woods, Brent, 33; *134*

Wounded Knee, SD, 53-54; 189

Wovoka, 53-54

Wyoming, 50; 52; 54-55; 78; 116; 131;
  134; 143; 153; 171; 187

Yellowstone Park, MT, *74*

Yorktown, VA, 12

Young, Charles,144; *145*; 145-46;
  147; 148; *175*; 181-82;

Zane Grey Theater, 196; 198

Zapata, Emiliano, 176

Zouave, 119

Zulu, 122-23

OTHER SCHIFFER BOOKS
BY THE AUTHOR

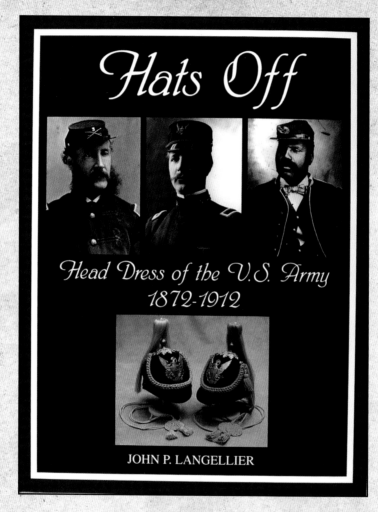

Hats Off
US Army Headgear, 1872-1902
978-0-7643-0956-4